In the quarter century since the publication of his *Arcades Project*, Walter Benjamin has become a decisive reference point for a whole range of critical disciplines. Benjamin constructed a unique and provocative synthesis of aesthetics, politics and philosophy. This volume of the *Thinkers for Architects* series assesses the significance of Benjamin's writings for architectural theory and practice.

Starting with the intertwining of life and work within Benjamin's writings on European cities, this book examines Benjamin's contributions to cultural criticism in relation to the works of Max Ernst, Adolf Loos, Le Corbusier and Sigfried Giedion and situates Benjamin's work within more recent developments in architecture and urbanism.

This book is a concise, coherent account of the relevance of Walter Benjamin's writings to architects, considering figures of modern art and architecture in detail, and locating Benjamin's critical work within the context of contemporary architecture and urbanism.

Brian Elliott currently teaches philosophy at Oregon State and Portland State University. His recent book *Constructing Community* (Rowman and Littlefield, 2010) is an exploration of three contemporary theories of community in light of currently influential approaches to urban development across liberal democracies.

Thinkers for Architects

Series Editor: Adam Sharr, Newcastle University, UK

Editorial board

Jonathan A. Hale, University of Nottingham, UK

Hilde Heynen, KU Leuven, Netherlands

David Leatherbarrow, University of Pennsylvania, USA

Architects have often looked to philosophers and theorists from beyond the discipline for design inspiration or in search of a critical framework for practice. This original series offers quick, clear introductions to key thinkers who have written about architecture and whose work can yield insights for designers.

Deleuze and Guattari for Architects

Andrew Ballantyne

Heidegger for Architects

Adam Sharr

Irigaray for Architects

Peg Rawes

Bhabha for Architects

Felipe Hernández

Bourdieu for Architects

Helena Webster

Benjamin for Architects

Brian Elliott

Derrida for Architects

Richard Coyne

Merleau-Ponty for Architects

Jonathan Hale

Benjamin

for

Architects

Brian Elliott

LONDON AND NEW YORK

First published 2011
by Routledge
2 Park Square, Milton Park, Abingdon, Oxon OX14 4RN

Simultaneously published in the USA and Canada
by Routledge
270 Madison Avenue, New York, NY 10016

Routledge is an imprint of the Taylor & Francis Group, an informa business

Typeset in Frutiger and Galliard by Wearset Ltd, Boldon, Tyne and Wear
Printed and bound in Great Britain by TJ International Ltd, Padstow,
Cornwall

British Library Cataloguing in Publication Data
A catalogue record for this book is available from the British Library

Library of Congress Cataloging-in-Publication Data
Elliott, Brian, 1969–
Benjamin for architects/Brian Elliott.
p. cm. – (Thinkers for architects; 6)
Includes bibliographical references and index.
1. Benjamin, Walter, 1892–1940. 2. Architecture–Philosophy. I.
Title.
B3209.B584E45 2010
720.1–dc22

                                        2010027629

ISBN13: 978-0-415-55814-3 (hbk)
ISBN13: 978-0-415-55815-0 (pbk)
ISBN13: 978-0-203-83387-2 (ebk)

For Gabrielle – my guide through the labyrinth

Contents

Series Editor's Preface

Adam Sharr

Architects have often looked to thinkers in philosophy and theory for design ideas, or in search of a critical framework for practice. Yet architects and students of architecture can struggle to navigate thinkers' writings. It can be daunting to approach original texts with little appreciation of their contexts. And existing introductions seldom explore architectural material in any detail. This original series offers clear, quick and accurate introductions to key thinkers who have written about architecture. Each book summarises what a thinker has to offer for architects. It locates their architectural thinking in the body of their work, introduces significant books and essays, helps decode terms and provides quick reference for further reading. If you find philosophical and theoretical writing about architecture difficult, or just don't know where to begin, this series will be indispensable.

Books in the *Thinkers for Architects* series come out of architecture. They pursue architectural modes of understanding, aiming to introduce a thinker to an architectural audience. Each thinker has a unique and distinctive ethos, and the structure of each book derives from the character at its focus. The thinkers explored are prodigious writers and any short introduction can only address a fraction of their work. Each author – an architect or an architectural critic – has focussed on a selection of a thinker's writings which they judge most relevant to designers and interpreters of architecture. Inevitably, much will be left out. These books will be the first point of reference, rather than the last word, about a particular thinker for architects. It is hoped that they will encourage you to read further; offering an incentive to delve deeper into the original writings of a particular thinker.

The *Thinkers for Architects* series has proved highly successful, expanding now to eight volumes dealing with familiar cultural figures whose writings have influenced architectural designers, critics and commentators in distinctive and important ways. Books explore the work of: Gilles Deleuze and Felix Guattari; Martin Heidegger; Luce Irigaray; Homi Bhabha; Pierre Bourdieu, Walter Benjamin; Jacques Derrida and Maurice Merleau-Ponty. The series continues to expand, addressing an increasingly rich diversity of contemporary thinkers who have something to say to architects.

Adam Sharr is Professor of Architecture at the University of Newcastle-upon-Tyne, Principal of Adam Sharr Architects and Editor (with Richard Weston) of *arq: Architectural Research Quarterly*, Cambridge University Press' international architecture journal. His books include *Heidegger for Architects*.

Acknowledgements

I have been afforded many opportunities to teach and present my ideas on Benjamin and architecture in recent years. A seminar on visual studies at Istanbul Bilgi University was made possible by the director of the cultural studies programme there, Ferda Keskin. My thanks to the graduate students at Bilgi for their enthusiasm and rigour. Also from that time my participation in *Istanbul Fragmented*, organized by Ipek Akpinar at Istanbul Technical University, allowed me to present my own excavations of the arcades of that city. At University College Dublin collaborations with Hugh Campbell, Douglas Smith and Gillian Pye building bridges between the humanities and architecture were an inspiration.

Since moving to the United States, the support of Andrew Cutrofello and Rob Gould has been essential and is much appreciated. Thanks to Brook Muller at the University of Oregon for providing comments on a first draft of the first three chapters. I owe a debt of gratitude also to Adam Sharr, the series editor, for having faith in the project. I thank Georgina Johnson-Cook at Routledge for her courteous and efficient help with getting the manuscript through to production.

Finally, the greatest thanks go to my wife, Gabrielle. She is my reason for being here and, in the words of Rilke, *Hiersein ist herrlich*.

Eugene, Oregon
Spring 2010

Introduction

Why should an architectural practitioner or educator be interested in the work of the German Jewish thinker Walter Benjamin? After all, by the time of his tragic death in 1940 Benjamin's published work – primarily as a literary critic – was known only to very restricted circles of European intellectuals. Unlike his contemporary Martin Heidegger, he had produced no groundbreaking philosophical study that resonated within academia and beyond. He had not been active in the early days of the Frankfurt School of Critical Theory in the 1920s and had in fact even failed in the rather modest ambition of becoming a university professor. Worse still, Benjamin devoted – many of his close friends at the time would have said 'wasted' – the final decade-and-a-half of his life on a project concerned with nineteenth-century Paris that set no material limits and proposed no clear theoretical goals.

And yet Benjamin is undoubtedly one of *the* thinkers on architecture and the urban condition of the twentieth century. Engagement with Benjamin's thinking has a number of things to offer the architectural practitioner and student: profound and nuanced reflections on modernity and modernism; detailed analyses of the social and political impact of the built environment; consideration of architecture as a crucial medium and repository for the intersection of personal and shared cultural memory; a sense of the politically and historically charged nature of meaning carried by the built environment. Above all, Benjamin's thinking raises the question of *intergenerational justice and responsibility in architecture*. With so much talk of sustainable approaches in architecture, Benjamin's concern for intergenerational justice is timely and of genuine relevance.

Benjamin is undoubtedly one of *the* thinkers on architecture

and the urban condition of the twentieth century.

Above all, Benjamin's thinking raises the question of _intergenerational justice and responsibility in architecture._ With so much talk of sustainable approaches in architecture, Benjamin's concern for intergenerational justice is timely and of genuine relevance.

While never an official member of the Institute of Social Research, Benjamin was financially supported by it and published some of his most important studies in its journal during the last few years of his life. Founded in Frankfurt in 1923, the Institute was initially inspired by Georg Lukács' Marxist work _History and Class Consciousness_ to pursue the goal of bringing philosophical inquiry together with empirical social research. Following an important essay by Max Horkheimer around the time of his assuming the role of director in 1930, the Frankfurt School's shared approach became known as 'Critical Theory'. Benjamin fits into the Critical Theory frame in spirit if not to the letter, in so far as he offers analyses of modern culture that contest prevailing, socially conservative interpretations. To cite one example, Benjamin's insights into the potentially emancipating effects of modern technology anticipate by several decades the idea of a possible society of collective, aesthetic play popularized by the Critical Theorist Herbert Marcuse in the 1960s. During Benjamin's lifetime, however, the most influential individuals in the Frankfurt School, Theodore Adorno and Horkheimer, expressed profound misgivings about his approach and, in particular, his theoretical methodology. To judge by the intensity of academic interest in Benjamin in recent decades, his unwillingness to fall into line with the theoretical orthodoxy pressed upon him by Adorno and others in the Frankfurt School has been vindicated. What is often startling about Benjamin's writing is how fresh and contemporary it seems. Unlike much twentieth-century theory, Benjamin's thinking still seems capable of pointing the way to the future, rather than back to a situation that has long since ceased to concern us.

What is often startling about Benjamin's writing is how fresh and contemporary it seems. Unlike much twentieth-century theory, Benjamin's thinking still seems capable of pointing the way to the future, rather than back to a situation that has long since ceased to concern us.

From his writings on cities such as Berlin, Moscow and Naples in the mid-1920s through to his obsessive reconstruction of Paris during the Second Empire in the last decade of his life, Benjamin's abiding preoccupation remained the social and cultural impact of modern urbanization. The range of sources culled for his mature work on Paris was astonishing: the poetry of Baudelaire and his contemporaries, the writings of Marx and Engels and earlier utopian socialists, nineteenth-century historians, city guides and biographies and a vast array of materials on the fashions and ephemera of everyday culture. In addition, Benjamin was a close observer of the artistic avant-garde in Paris in his own time, paying particular attention to the significance of the surrealist group that formed around André Breton in the early 1920s. Above all, he drew inspiration from the pioneering urban sociology of Georg Simmel's 1903 essay, 'The Metropolis and Mental Life', in pursuing the question of the social effects of modern urbanization. Whereas Simmel accentuated the nervous exhaustion of the metropolitan 'blasé' character, Benjamin tended to read the urban environment with an eye for its socially transformative, revolutionary potential. While Benjamin's preoccupation with nineteenth-century Paris can seem rather remote from the core concerns of contemporary architecture, it should be borne in mind that his ultimate goal was to reconstruct the material and cultural conditions of the birth of modern urban life. In a word, Benjamin's underlying task was a *genealogy of urbanization*. All roads of this genealogy led back to the unparalleled urban renewal of Paris orchestrated by Baron Haussmann in the 1850s and 1860s.

Benjamin's underlying task was a *genealogy of urbanization*.

Haussmann's urban experiment would set in train further efforts at large-scale redevelopment throughout Europe and beyond. Here we find the model for all subsequent efforts to engineer society through modern construction. Benjamin, examining these developments several generations later, is gripped with the task of thinking through this seminal event in modernity. Rather than calmly distanced art-historical reconstruction, Benjamin's work on the *Passagen-Werk*, or *Arcades Project* (truly a work in progress in every sense of the term), was driven by an increasing sense of social and political urgency. He was convinced, as were the leading advocates of architectural modernism in the 1920s, that the only way forward lay in exploiting rather than suppressing the industrial technology pioneered in the nineteenth century. But if the body of modernity was its material technological innovations, its spirit drew from deeper sources. Like his contemporary and friend Ernst Bloch, Benjamin was convinced that nineteenth-century modernity and twentieth-century modernism were driven by collective utopian wish-images: largely unconscious desires for social harmony and reconciliation. Understanding modern architecture, therefore, could never be reduced to giving functional accounts of material applications and the economies of scale made possible by standardized production. Beyond any functionalist-expressionist dichotomy, Benjamin understands modern

Taking stock of the contemporary situation, it seems that the exhaustion of postmodern alternatives has led to a reassessment of what came before the 'post': the question of the meaning of modernism has returned. There could be no better guide to help us address this question than Walter Benjamin.

architecture as equally material-functional and symbolic-utopian. Taking stock of the contemporary situation, it seems that the exhaustion of postmodern alternatives has led to a reassessment of what came before the 'post': the question of the meaning of modernism has returned. There could be no better guide to help us address this question than Walter Benjamin.

Between April and July 2006, the Victoria and Albert Museum in London staged the exhibition *Modernism: Designing a New World, 1914–1939*. The following year the slightly modified exhibition transferred to the Corcoran Gallery of Art in Washington, DC. What was striking about what was described by the Corcoran as 'the largest and most comprehensive exhibition on the subject ever staged in America' was the clear focus on everyday material culture and architectural design, as opposed to the more orthodox preoccupation with the visual arts, particularly painting. The V&A online description – in a distinctly modernist tenor – accentuates the continued presence of modernism:

> At the beginning of the twenty-first century our relationship to Modernism is complex. The built environment that we live in today was largely shaped by Modernism. The buildings we inhabit, the chairs we sit on, the graphic design that surrounds us have all been created by the aesthetics and the ideology of Modernist design. We live in an era that still identifies itself in terms of Modernism, as post-Modernist or even post-post-Modernist (www.vam.ac.uk/vastatic/microsites/ 1331_modernism).

This characterization of modernism, not so much in terms of great individuals or even the bewildering array of -isms, but rather as something that is written into everyday material culture in a largely implicit manner, is profoundly in accord with Benjamin's sense of it. One of the key tasks of this book will be to draw out the complexity of Benjamin's appreciation of modernism in light of its continued relevance to contemporary architectural and intellectual culture.

The approach of this book is broadly thematic, though it also follows a loose chronological order. While the discussion covers a variety of periods and texts, the focus is for the most part on Benjamin's mature thinking from the 1930s.

Any consideration of Benjamin's relevance to architecture will draw heavily on the *Arcades Project* (AP). Benjamin's best-known works – such as his essay 'The Artwork in the Age of Mechanical Reproducibility' – can be adequately understood only through familiarity with the AP. This gives rise to a major problem: the AP is an intentionally fragmentary text consciously constructed following the methods of modern film montage. In addition, it is largely made up of material from other sources and only a small proportion of the text actually originates from Benjamin. Adorno complained in letters to his friend of Benjamin's obstinate desire to refrain from explicit theoretical construction. While acknowledging the genuine reasons for Benjamin's restraint in this regard, it is also true that a theory of architecture and urban experience can only be drawn from Benjamin's thinking through extrapolation and *construction*. Any such construction will resemble the reconstruction of a crime scene, bringing together seemingly circumstantial evidence into a compelling and coherent narrative.

While not suppressing the eclecticism of Benjamin's thinking, the attempt has been made here to identify a core idea with respect to architecture. This is *the shift from bourgeois dwelling to modernist housing*. The idea is found repeatedly in a variety of Benjamin's writings from the early 1930s across both published and unpublished sources. It appears to articulate a personal experience stemming from Benjamin's childhood, an experience that in various ways prefigured and coloured his later encounters with urban environments. But the shift from dwelling to housing was also something many of Benjamin's intellectual contemporaries would have recognized as a part of their tenuous position as a class. The subtitle

While not suppressing the eclecticism of Benjamin's thinking, the attempt has been made here to identify a core idea with respect to architecture. This is *the shift from bourgeois dwelling to modernist housing.*

of Benjamin's 1929 essay on surrealism refers to the movement as 'the last snapshot of the European intelligentsia'. Accordingly, the decay of dwelling can be seen as a crisis affecting the social existence of the intellectual class, a class to which artists and architects also belonged. Finally, the shift can be taken to refer to the explicit task of architectural modernism to replace the stiflingly decorated refuge of the Victorian bourgeois home with the stripped-down simplicity of the 'machine-house'. This would represent the effective reconciliation of humanity with the products of industrial technology, thereby ending the reactionary opposition to such technology as inherently dehumanizing.

The decay of dwelling can be seen as a crisis affecting the social existence of the intellectual class, a class to which artists and architects also belonged.

In accordance with the centrality accorded to the shift from dwelling to housing in Benjamin's thinking, Chapter 1 begins with his autobiographical recollections of the domestic interiors of his sheltered, upper-middle-class childhood and moves on to consider his writings on cities such as Naples and Moscow, encountered as a young man. Whereas in Naples Benjamin grasps the openness of a Mediterranean working-class culture as an antidote to northern European domestic isolation, in Moscow he confronts a metropolis under the full force of revolutionary modernist reconstruction. Clearly opposed to the valorization of pre-industrial, rural dwelling found in a thinker such as Heidegger, Benjamin affirms the progressive social potential of architectural modernism. Here the sweeping away of the excessive furnishings of the bourgeois domestic interior of the nineteenth century is seen as producing an exhilarating sense of social and moral emancipation. The liberated interiors of modernist architectural design allow for an effective manner of exorcizing the nightmares of nineteenth-century history.

After exploring Benjamin's move towards a version of revolutionary Marxism in Chapter 2, the modernist liberation of the built environment is explored through

Clearly opposed to the valorization of pre-industrial, rural dwelling found in a thinker such as Heidegger, Benjamin affirms the progressive social potential of architectural modernism. ... The liberated interiors of modernist architectural design allow for an effective manner of exorcizing the nightmares of nineteenth-century history.

tensions between surrealism and purism in Chapter 3. Tying in with the work of Manfredo Tafuri from the 1970s and more recent studies by the urban sociologist David Harvey, Chapter 4 focuses on the utopian dimension of modern architecture. Rejecting the heroic characterization of the artist/architect as solitary genius, Benjamin invites us to consider the products of architectural design as manifestations of collective visions of the good life. While Benjamin is under no illusions about how compromised such visions become under capitalist economic conditions, he insists that traces of collective utopian projections can always be found by genuine efforts to think through architectural plans and realizations. In Chapter 5 the contribution of Benjamin's thinking to the problem of public participation in architecture is examined. While the explicit ideology of architectural modernism has often been regarded as authoritarian and essentially opposed to popular participation, Benjamin tends to read it against the grain of this ideology. What makes Benjamin's engagement with modern architecture genuine and productive is the fact that he does not see it as reducible to its ideological function.

Benjamin's dialectical appreciation of architecture stands equally opposed to any reductive environment determinism or non-materialist idealism. In theory at least this would align Benjamin with contemporary approaches to urban ecology. But Benjamin ties *revolutionary social change* to valid artistic and constructive activity. In his famous text 'On the Concept of History' he strongly defends the revolutionary demand and thus sets against Le Corbusier's implacable disjunction 'Architecture or Revolution' the conjunction 'Architecture *and* Revolution'. In more specific terms, Benjamin's thinking can be understood to address the question of architectural agency. This question, which arose most insistently and conspicuously within professional architecture under the conditions of world economic crisis in the 1970s, is implicitly in play in all of Benjamin's writings on art and the urban condition. His own positive vision of artistic production – articulated most clearly in the essay 'The Author as Producer' – involves the breakdown of any strict division between producer and consumer. Cashing this thought out in relation to architecture, it points to a situation in which all members of a community actively contribute in some way to the conditions of their own housing. Such an approach appears to be in tune with a contemporary sensibility that is increasingly shaped by a concern for small-scale communities and regional sustainability. While Benjamin's writings are obviously not the place to look for specific proposals for grassroots community housing, he can help us to think through the full implications of the modernist revolution in construction that was spearheaded by architects, as well as the anti- and postmodernist alternatives of more recent decades. Prefiguring later 'psychogeographical' approaches to the urban environment in the 1960s, Benjamin offers a street-level perspective of the city to balance the psychological abstraction and distance induced by computer modelling and the architectural studio.

Prefiguring later 'psychogeographical' approaches to the urban environment in the 1960s, Benjamin offers a street-level perspective of the city to balance the psychological abstraction and distance induced by computer modelling and the architectural studio.

In sum, anyone concerned with architecture in all its historical, cultural, social, and political significance and complexity cannot fail to learn much of contemporary relevance from studying the work of Walter Benjamin. His analyses of modern cities and of seminal modernist movements, along with his ideas of intergenerational justice, the social effects of modern technology and the progressive potential of modern construction, all give his writings a contemporary resonance which is unsurpassed among twentieth-century European thinkers. If, as Jürgen Habermas insisted in the 1980s, modernity is an 'unfinished project', no thinker is better equipped than Benjamin to offer the contemporary architect the means to engage with and articulate a condition of modernity that is yet to have run its course.

CHAPTER 1

Metropolitanism and Method

Childhood images

In 'Berlin Childhood around 1900' Benjamin remarks: 'the images of my metropolitan childhood perhaps are capable, at their core, of preforming later historical experience' (Benjamin 2002: 344). Only a writer as attuned to the particularities of his material environment as Benjamin could qualify so profound an experience by a tentative 'perhaps'. As we shall see, the idea that historical experience (both for the individual and collectively) is made possible through images attached to material objects comes to dominate Benjamin's thinking increasingly over the course of his life. Undoubtedly, this idea is intimately connected with a heightened sense of the precariousness of those material places in which the writer had grown up as a child and inhabited as a mature man.

In this opening chapter we will consider the metropolitan sites that shaped Benjamin's experience and thinking. In a way that would come to be explicitly stated in his late writings, for Benjamin biography is essentially topography: the writing of a life inextricably tied up with writing about the places of that life. The writings on cities, however, should not be considered as merely personal documents. Crucially, they are also documents of a metropolitan experience that writers of literature and theory had struggled to articulate for over 100 years before Benjamin's own attempts. The unprecedented growth of cities across industrially developed nations in the nineteenth century had given rise to equally unprecedented social dynamics. In addition to his finely tuned metropolitan sensibility, Benjamin was intimately acquainted with modern urban history, literature and theory. Ultimately, he came to see his own personal development in light of collective social and political conditions stemming from the modern history of the city. Benjamin addresses this history at a time when one of the pioneering figures of European architectural modernism, Le Corbusier, could insist on the dramatic alternative: 'architecture or revolution'.

For Benjamin biography is essentially topography: the writing of a life inextricably tied up with writing about the places of that life.

Before considering the series of essays Benjamin published on various cities in the 1920s, it is necessary to gain a provisional sense of his theoretical methodology. Benjamin was far removed from being a wide-eyed, naive recorder of urban impressions. Instead, his writings on cities are motivated by a profound desire for personal and collective redemption and expressed in a richly allusive style made possible by his intimate and comprehensive acquaintance with literature and theory. Following notions found in the work of such influential literary contemporaries as Hugo von Hoffmannsthal, Rainer Maria Rilke and Marcel Proust, Benjamin proceeds on the premise that, for the writer, redemption requires working through childhood memories (see Rochlitz 1996: 181–7). The basic idea here is that of 'preformation' mentioned in the opening citation. Recollecting childhood for Benjamin means attempting to find the meaning of one's present situation in light of a promise implicitly expressed in former years. In a word, memory becomes the primary space of historical meaning. While this may appear initially as an exclusively personal and subjective process, in view of the fact that Benjamin grasps memories as essentially connected to the material environment, recollection in fact has intrinsically social and historical dimensions. Recollecting one's childhood home, for example, will be differently coloured depending on whether the actual physical structure survives the child's transition into adulthood. Physical survival, however, is only one factor in recollection. The styles, furnishings and surroundings of the childhood home are also of central significance. As we shall see, Benjamin was particularly sensitive to processes of decay and obsolescence within the physical environment. In his mature work in the 1930s he came to analyse this process in terms of the Marxian notion of commodity fetishism. Early modernist architecture also focused on the phenomenon of obsolescence and attempted to confront it by overcoming the nineteenth-century preoccupation with styles. Such a solution could not be adequate from Benjamin's perspective, as generating distinctive styles is an imperative of commodity production in conjunction with mass advertising. While modernist architecture could not, therefore, offer Benjamin an adequate material solution to the problem of obsolescence, it nevertheless contained a utopian impulse of great value. This impulse will be considered in Chapter 4.

Benjamin was particularly sensitive to processes of decay and obsolescence within the physical environment. In his mature work in the 1930s he came to analyse this process in terms of the Marxian notion of commodity fetishism.

Following collaborative work with his friend Franz Hessel translating Marcel Proust's *In Search of Lost Time*, Benjamin offered his first published reflections on its author in the 1929 essay 'On the Image of Proust'. Here Benjamin remarks: 'It took Proust to make the nineteenth century ripe for memoirs. What before him had been a period devoid of tension now became a force field in which later writers aroused multifarious currents' (Benjamin 1999a: 240). Notions that preoccupied Benjamin at the time find their way into this essay: the idea of coming to terms with modern history through comedy rather than tragedy; the reality of the nineteenth century as a 'satanic fairyland'; and a concept of history as a two-sided dialectic of melancholic and rejuvenating recollection. Benjamin relates Proust's work to the second side of that dialectic and speaks of an 'elegiac idea of happiness ... which for Proust transforms existence into a preserve of memory' (239). As the title of Proust's great work makes clear, the author's primary concern relates to *time*. The early episodes of *In Search of Lost Time* depict childhood experiences of dream and recollection and thus point to two instances of image consciousness. Proust's notion of the image is ultimately related to time experienced as a kind of density, as something object-like, rather than as a neutral measure of events. As Benjamin remarks:

> **The eternity which Proust opens to view is intertwined time, not boundless time. His true interest is in the passage of time in its most real – that is, intertwined – form, and this passage nowhere holds sway more openly than in remembrance within and aging without (244).**

The key significance of the Proust essay to Benjamin's thinking is encapsulated in a simple formula: 'Proust's method is actualization, not reflection [*Nicht Reflexion – Vergegenwärtigung ist Prousts Verfahren*]' (ibid., see also Benjamin 1991: 320). The German term translated as 'actualization' – *Vergegenwärtigung* – means literally 'to make present'. Thus, in Proust's writing the image acts so as to bring past experience into the present. It does this 'in a flash' (*blitzhaft*): 'Proust has brought off the monstrous feat of letting the whole world age in an instant' (Benjamin 1999a: 244). The achievement of the image is accordingly 'to charge an entire lifetime with the utmost mental awareness [*Geistesgegenwart*]' (ibid.). As opposed to the daydreams that inhabit the landscape of fairy tales, the literary image is thus a function of concentration and presence of mind. In a word, such images redeem a life by rendering the past critically meaningful in the living present.

As is clear across many of Benjamin's writings, his encounter with Proust is as much an attempt to clarify his own experience as it is an exercise in sophisticated interpretation and appreciation. Benjamin's attempts to recollect his own childhood should thus be viewed in light of his reflections on Proust. These reflections establish two methodological principles that structure the development of Benjamin's thinking: first, that the meaning of the present is latent within the past; and, second, that this meaning can only be made explicit through recollecting the material environment in which past experience is embedded. The more precise meaning of this process of recovery can be clarified by considering Benjamin's writings on cities.

Berlin

In many respects Benjamin enjoyed near perfect conditions for a child growing up in Berlin at the end of the nineteenth century. His parents both came from financially secure upper-middle-class families and after their marriage they maintained a stable position. Walter was the first born, with a brother and sister following him. The portrayal of 'Berlin Childhood around 1900' (written 1932–4 and revised in 1938) begins with a sense of protective seclusion offered by the courtyard onto which his family's apartment looked. As Benjamin points out in 'Berlin Chronicle' (completed in 1932), his family history in Berlin stretched back only as far as his grandparents, who had originally settled in the city in the mid-nineteenth century. For the young Benjamin, however, this limited history was sufficient to endue his maternal grandmother's apartment with 'the almost immemorial feeling of bourgeois security' (Benjamin 2002: 369). In 'Berlin Childhood' Benjamin alludes to his particular attraction to the loggia of his grandmother's apartment. This is significant in view of Benjamin's obsessive interest in the Paris arcades that came to dominate the last decade-and-a-half of his life. The description of the loggia contains clues for understanding this connection:

> The most important of these secluded rooms [in my grandmother's apartment] was for me the loggia. This may have been because it was more modestly furnished and hence less appreciated by the adults, or because muted street noise would carry up there, or because it offered me a view of the courtyard with porters, children, and organ grinders. At any rate, it was the voices more than the forms that one noticed from the loggia ... Sunday – which the other rooms, as though worn out, could never quite retain, for it seeped right through them – Sunday was contained in the loggia alone, which looked out onto the courtyard, with its rails for hanging carpets, and out onto other loggias; and no vibration of the burden of bells, with which the Church of the Twelve Apostles and St Matthew's would load it, ever slipped off, but all remained stored up in it till evening (Benjamin 2002: 371).

Benjamin's account offers pertinent starting points for coming to appreciate his experience of buildings and the built environment more generally. The form and function of the loggia stand out from those of other rooms of the nineteenth-century European middle-class apartment. This is primarily in view of the fact that it is the one place where the outside penetrates the inside to any significant degree. Benjamin is clearly describing a fully covered rather than open loggia, which would be obviously less suited to the climate of northern Europe. Two senses are privileged in the loggia: sight and hearing. In terms of sight, it offers the best opportunities for viewing the courtyard with its 'genteel' activities and parade of characters. Presumably the use of glass was more conspicuous and intense in the loggia than in other rooms, which were more concerned to distract attention away from the world beyond the apartment.

It is the aural qualities of the room, however, that are most emphasized. In particular, the way in which the sound of the church bells gathers and settles in the loggia makes a powerful impression. It is worthwhile noting that, in the earlier 'Berlin Chronicle', Benjamin draws attention to his poor visual sense and speaks of 'a gaze that appears to see not a third of what it takes in' (Benjamin 2002: 596). This limited vision, together with a poor sense of direction, combined to produce what he calls there 'a period of impotence before the city' (ibid.). In an important sense, therefore, Benjamin's biography describes the construction of a map not meant for the eye. It is important to bear this in mind when appreciating his attempt to come to terms with the metropolitan condition. Though he grew up in the metropolis he clearly did not feel equal to it in childhood. Only in Paris, as we shall see, did Benjamin's optical limitations finally give way to a positive, more

Benjamin's biography describes the construction of a map not meant for the eye. It is important to bear this in mind when appreciating his attempt to come to terms with the metropolitan condition. Though he grew up in the metropolis he clearly did not feel equal to it in childhood.

visceral rapport with the urban environment. This achievement can be seen as foreshadowed by the child's affinity with the loggia.

The text most intimately connected with Benjamin's move from Berlin to Paris is *One-Way Street*. Written between 1923 and 1926 but not published until 1928, *One-Way Street* immediately stands out on account of its formal novelty. Arranged into short fragments bearing ambiguous titles drawn from everyday advertisements and signs, here Benjamin for the first time puts his technique of montage to work as a new mode of theoretical writing. An extended section called 'Imperial Panorama' is made up of some of the earliest composed material. The first clue for interpreting this part of the text is offered by the title. The *Kaiserpanorama* or Imperial Panorama was constructed in Berlin in the early 1870s and situated within an arcade (see Buck-Morss 1989: 82–92). For a small charge it offered the public the opportunity of individually viewing photographic images of distant sites and cities. Viewers were situated around the machine, thus facing each other while remaining individually absorbed in enjoyment of the images displayed. Benjamin writes in 'Berlin Childhood' of visiting it as a young boy and relates his experience of the anxiety induced when a bell rang announcing an imminent change of picture.

Whereas his later writings on the German metropolis have a more elegiac tone, 'Imperial Panorama' strives from the outset to convey a powerful impression of the social corruption at work in the German capital city: 'In the stock phraseology that lays bare the amalgam of stupidity and cowardice constituting the mode of life of the German bourgeois, the locution referring to impending catastrophe – "Things can't go on like this" – is particularly noteworthy' (Benjamin 1996: 451). In contrast to the account of everyday life in Naples he will write a year later, the German city presents a situation in which 'circumstances, squalor, and stupidity here subjugate people entirely to collective forces, as the lives of savages alone are subjected to tribal laws' (Benjamin 1996: 453). In a particularly noteworthy passage, Benjamin's experience of Berlin, with its 'heavy curtain that shuts off Germany's sky', prompts an account of the city as corrupt, deformed and barbarous:

Just as all things, in an irreversible process of mingling and contamination, are losing their intrinsic character while ambiguity displaces authenticity, so is the city. Great cities ... are seen to be breached at all points by the invading countryside. Not by the landscape, but by what is bitterest in untrammeled nature: ploughed land, highways, night sky that the veil of vibrant redness no longer conceals. The insecurity of even the busy areas puts the city dweller in the opaque and truly dreadful situation in which he must assimilate, along with isolated monstrosities from the open country, the abortions of urban architectonics (Benjamin 1996: 454).

While in isolation it is difficult to pin down the specific object of Benjamin's complaint here, broader consideration of the text as a whole makes it clear that the tension between nature and technology is centrally in play. While the final entry of 'Imperial Panorama' speaks of a failed sense of appreciation for 'Mother Earth', the very final section of *One-Way Street* sees modern technology as giving rise to a new configuration of nature 'through which mankind's contact with the cosmos takes a new and different form from that which it had in nations and families' (Benjamin 1996: 487). When such connections are made it becomes clear that, already by 1923, Benjamin was identifying the intersection of modern technology and urban experience as a key site of historical tension. While figures such as Le Corbusier focused on what was to be overcome in

Already by 1923, Benjamin was identifying the intersection of modern technology and urban experience as a key site of historical tension. While figures such as Le Corbusier focused on what was to be overcome in realizing the 'New Spirit' of construction, Benjamin clearly saw that the past could not be transcended with such ease.

realizing the 'New Spirit' of construction, Benjamin clearly saw that the past could not be transcended with such ease.

In the same year as his major essay on surrealism appeared (1929), Benjamin published a review of Franz Hessel's *Walking in Berlin* (*Spazieren in Berlin*) under the title 'The Return of the Flâneur'. Hessel, Benjamin's collaborator on the Proust translation, is credited with writing an account of Berlin to rival the surrealist Louis Aragon's *Paris Peasant* from a few years earlier. While Aragon had haunted the Passage de l'Opéra, evoking the historical tensions of a material site characterized by its descent into obsolescence and destitution, Hessel is seen as tracking down the remaining traces of metropolitan dwelling on the eve of a decisive transformation:

> the cult of 'dwelling' in the old sense, with the idea of security at its core, has now received its death knell. Giedion, Mendelssohn, and Le Corbusier are converting human habitations into transitional spaces of every imaginable force and wave of light and air. ... Only a man in whom modernity has already announced its presence, however quietly, can cast such an original and 'early' glance at what has only just become old (Benjamin 1999a: 264).

This is a decisive early reference in Benjamin's writings to the decay of 'dwelling' related explicitly to the rise of modernist architecture. In the present context it is a question of appreciating how this shift from dwelling to modernist housing was woven into Benjamin's biographical construction of his own personal and intellectual development. In 'Berlin Chronicle' Benjamin names Hessel as a later guide that helped him overcome his powerlessness in the face of the metropolis. As a first stage in this process Benjamin speaks of the 'Tiergarten mythology' as

It is a question of appreciating how this shift from dwelling to modernist housing was woven into Benjamin's biographical construction of his own personal and intellectual development.

'the first chapter of a science of this city' (Benjamin 1999a: 599). Used as a deer park until the eighteenth century – whence the name – the Tiergarten district of Berlin has a labyrinthine structure that Benjamin takes up as his dominant 'thought figure' (in German *Denkbild*) for the modern metropolis. The ancient Greek myth of the labyrinth, wherein Theseus faces the threat of the Minotaur lying at the centre of the maze and then follows Ariadne's thread to find his way out, features from the outset in Benjamin's description of Berlin. But it is only through his experience of Paris that he finally achieves a rapport equal to the metropolis. Such a rapport is described not in terms of mastery but instead as *surrender* to the metropolitan environment:

> Not to find one's way in a city may well be uninteresting and banal. It requires ignorance – nothing more. But to lose oneself in a city – as one loses oneself in a forest – this calls for quite a different schooling ... Paris taught me this art of straying; it fulfilled a dream that had shown its first traces in the labyrinths on the blotting pages of my school exercise books (Benjamin 1999a: 598).

Before Benjamin truly found himself in Paris, however, the move from Berlin brought with it important diversions to Naples and Moscow. Benjamin's experience of these cities marks respectively the beginning and end of a decisive period of transformation in his appreciation and articulation of urban experience. At the professional level, Benjamin makes the decision (to a great extent forced upon him) to abandon a career in academia and pursue one as an essayist and journalist. This brings with it an intensified interest in and affinity with the ephemeral and contemporary. His writings on cities from this period of the mid-1920s convey the celebratory and emancipating spirit of the urban condition. While the figure of the solitary and alienated flâneur will never be far away, here the city is above all an environment of vibrant collective existence. In this way, the twentieth-century city comes to stand directly opposed to the stifling isolation of the nineteenth-century bourgeois interior of Benjamin's youth.

Naples

Benjamin's essay 'Naples' was written together with the Latvian dramaturge and committed communist Asja Lacis. Following the breakdown of his marriage several years earlier, Benjamin began a relationship with Lacis while in Italy during the summer of 1924 (see Scholem 1981: 146–57; Buck-Morss 1989: 8–24). The essay is the first of a series explicitly focused on and named after cities and as such represents a turning point in Benjamin's approach to theoretical writing, a transition that will be announced more stridently with the publication of *One-Way Street*. Certain tendencies and ideas that feature in his later accounts of Berlin appear for the first time in the 'Naples' essay. Chief among these is a fine attunement to urban architecture in so far as it mediates domestic and public space. The dominant idea of the essay is the *porosity* of the Neapolitan urban environment:

> Porosity results not only from the indolence of the southern artisan, but also, above all, from the passion for improvisation, which demands that space and opportunity be preserved at any price. Buildings are used as a popular stage.... What is enacted on the staircases is an advanced school of stage management. The stairs, never entirely exposed, but still less enclosed in the gloomy box of the Nordic house, erupt fragmentarily from the buildings, make an angular turn, and disappear, only to burst out again (Benjamin 1996: 416–17).

Here two features of porosity are made explicit: improvisation and theatricality. Both features bring to mind a key dialectical tension that comes to accompany the development of architecture from the 1920s on. Predicated on standardization and comprehensive design, modernist architecture and urbanism encountered early on the problems of localized modification and popular participation. Le Corbusier, for example, was already allowing for limited reconfiguration of domestic interiors in his designs of the late 1920s, through such innovations as movable room divisions. According to Manfredo Tafuri and Francesco Dal Co, this period in Le Corbusier's development involves a decisive move towards a method of *montage* in projects for São Paulo, Rio de Janeiro, Montevideo and Algiers:

Montage presupposes the programming of the individual elements – in this case cells that in theory can be moved about, dismantled, and set up elsewhere – within a fixed structure conceived on a territorial scale. Each cell can be replaced without altering the nature of the program, without contradicting the overall form. ... Active participation is expected of the public using it: the maximum freedom made possible by the *terrains artificiels* – freestanding platforms that, within the serpentine-shaped structure, would provide ample space to be filled eventually with residential cells – would enable the public to become protagonists in the construction of the city and in its consumption (Tafuri and Dal Co 1979: 143).

This concession to popular participation in architectural design was, however, extremely modest when compared to those insisted upon as the challenge to modernist orthodoxy gained momentum in the 1960s. Seen as an anticipation of such movements, 'Naples' celebrates an urban vibrancy stemming from the creative chaos of localized modification and the lack of any standardized, comprehensive urban plan. In opposition to another key element of the modernist paradigm, the functional separation of domestic and retail structures, Naples is found to flourish on account of a thorough mixing of functions. Rather than the elegance and convenience of the modern department store that stands aloof from its surrounding environment and strives to be a world unto itself, commerce in this Mediterranean city takes place in a mobile, labyrinthine space of play:

Blissful confusion in the storehouses! For here they are still one with the vendors' stalls: they are bazaars. The long passageway is favored. In a glass-roofed one, there is a toyshop (in which perfume and liqueur glasses are

'Naples' celebrates an urban vibrancy stemming from the creative chaos of localized modification and the lack of any standardized, comprehensive urban plan.

also on sale) that would hold its own beside fairy-tale galleries. Like a gallery, too, is the main street of Naples, the Toledo. Its traffic is among the densest on earth. On either side of this narrow alley, all that has come together in the harbor city lies insolently, crudely, seductively displayed. Only in fairy tales are lanes so long that one must pass through without looking left or right, if one is to avoid falling prey to the devil (Benjamin 1996: 419).

Just as northern European domestic seclusion is contrasted with a southern tendency to bring private life into public space as a kind of theatre, the communal character of the poorer districts of Naples is opposed to the reclusive spaces of bourgeois life. Such is the centrifugal force of the Neapolitan working-class domestic interior that the few items of furniture it contains find themselves out on the street. While there is obviously a certain romanticizing of what are more plausibly understood as functional necessities, it is still worth noting how Benjamin here anticipates another feature of the critique of modernist urbanism.

As Jane Jacobs' was the first to make explicit in *The Death and Life of Great American Cities*, urban density and functional mixture naturally give rise to 'eyes on the street' that enhance a sense of urban cohabitation and security (Jacobs 1993). The 'Naples' essay insists on the positive value of not just eyes, but whole bodies – together with their domestic furnishings – on the street. This suggests in turn a mode of everyday urban living with a strong tendency to erupt into festival at any time: 'Irresistibly, the festival penetrates each and every working day. Porosity is the inexhaustible law of life in this city, reappearing everywhere' (Benjamin 1996: 417). In this way, the image of Naples as a city of play is underscored. The traditional festival or carnival also has a more politically charged meaning, in so far as it represents an overturning of the social hierarchy that structures the city under the normal conditions of productive work. Again, whereas the functional urbanism of the modernist paradigm insists on strict separation of productive and recreational areas, Naples transforms the environment of work into one of play given the slightest pretext.

While Berlin for the young Benjamin represented a labyrinth in which his poor vision allowed for little meaningful movement, Naples offered the experience of a maze within which he could begin to lose himself in a positive, liberating sense. In 1923 Benjamin's sense of personal claustrophobia in the German capital, combined with the generalized social misery brought on by hyperinflation, caused him to connect all hope for genuine productivity with his escape from Berlin. Shortly before his departure for Capri in the spring of 1924, he wrote to his friend Gerhard (later Gershom) Scholem in connection with his ongoing work on an academic study of the mourning play (*Trauerspiel*):

> **At the beginning of April I intend – by hook or by crook – to get away from here and, to the extent that it is in my power, to complete this matter from a somewhat superior vantage point and quickly, under the benign influence of a more relaxed life in more spacious and freer surroundings (Scholem and Adorno 1994: 236).**

As noted, his intensely negative experience of the German capital in the years following the First World War was recorded in *One-Way Street*. Benjamin dedicated this text to Lacis: 'This street is named Asja Lacis Street after her who as a engineer cut it through the author' (Benjamin 1996: 444). The language of the dedication should be taken seriously, in so far as it expresses the violent and visceral transformation of Benjamin's approach to writing and criticism at this time. There are many dimensions to this transformation. One is the movement from academia to journalism precipitated by the ultimate failure of Benjamin's study of the mourning play to find acceptance by a university assessment board. Without the higher doctoral degree or *Habilitation* attained through such a process, Benjamin could not pursue a career as a university professor. Second, in terms of political perspective, Lacis prompted Benjamin to take seriously the Marxian critique of bourgeois culture and society. These two factors in conjunction lead Benjamin to reconsider his mode of writing and his critical-theoretical position in a profound and lasting manner.

Whereas his early writings are characterized by extreme conceptual density and an abstract, rather hermetic style, *One-Way Street* announces a form of writing that strives to correspond explicitly to everyday urban experience. As the opening section, 'Filling Station', proclaims:

> Significant literary effectiveness can come into being only in a strict
> alternation between action and writing; it must nurture the inconspicuous
> forms that fit its influence in active communities better than it does the
> pretentious, universal gesture of the book – in leaflets, brochures, articles,
> and placards. Only this prompt language shows itself equal to the moment
> (Benjamin 1996: 444).

In a letter to Scholem from May 1926, written during his preparation of
One-Way Street for publication, Benjamin speaks of a transition in his political
position from anarchism to communism. At the same time he insists that this
transition concerns methods rather than goals, declaring communist goals to be
'nonsense and nonexistent' (Scholem and Adorno 1994: 301). In a further letter
to Scholem written several months later Benjamin insists that the title of the text
should *not* be understood metaphorically and that it refers to 'a street that is
meant to reveal a prospect of such precipitous depth … like, perhaps, Palladio's
famous design in Vincenza, *The Street*' (306). Palladio's *Teatro Olimpico*, to
which Benjamin refers here, is the sole surviving example of a Renaissance
theatre construction. The theatre features set designs of street scenes realized
later by Vincenzo Scamozzi, an influential architectural theorist from the final
period of the Italian Renaissance. Giving a powerful impression of heightened
reality, these sets utilized contemporary technologies to provide foreshortened
perspectives through tilted floors and contracted ceiling angles.

Benjamin's comparison between his new mode of writing and the Renaissance
theatre can be understood through reference to methodological comments that
were written later in the context of the *Arcades Project*. In one significant
remark Benjamin speaks of striving to 'conjoin a heightened graphicness
[*Anschaulichkeit*] to the realization of Marxist method' (1999b: 461). Benjamin's
literary method thus attempts a kind of verbal *trompe l'œil* in the sense that it
strives to make its subjects more immediate and striking to the reader. At the
same time, however, Benjamin is not ultimately appealing to aesthetic illusion in
its traditional sense. For the construction of the image in Benjamin is always
geared towards transformative action, whereas aesthetic illusion is traditionally
understood to disengage the viewer from action.

Benjamin's literary method thus attempts a kind of verbal *trompe l'œil* in the sense that it strives to make its subjects more immediate and striking to the reader.

Although Benjamin would not definitively leave Berlin until 1933, when the political situation seemed quite hopeless, his flight from the city a decade before and decisive relationship with Lacis marked the point at which the place would no longer be the primary site of his struggles. The culturally and politically conservative forces that had shaped his intellectual development in Germany were suddenly and irrevocably turned on their head with Benjamin's absorption of Lacis' commitment to revolutionary communism. While his future work would remain far from conventional commentary or orthodox theory in the eyes of his later Frankfurt School admirers and critics, a certain alignment with the 'modern spirit' is undoubtedly in evidence from the mid-1920s on. His encounters with the Mediterranean city in the spring and summer of 1924 were critical for Benjamin's subsequent commitment to and sympathy with everyday urban existence.

Moscow

After completing *One-Way Street* but prior to its delayed publication, Benjamin travelled to Moscow in the winter of 1926–7. One immediate reason for the trip was his desire to see Lacis, who was at the time recuperating in a sanatorium. Also of importance was the chance of experiencing at first hand the character of the metropolis under post-revolutionary conditions. He had received an advance to write an essay on his experience of Soviet Russia upon his return to Berlin and to this end maintained a detailed diary throughout the two months of his stay in Moscow. In his preface to the German publication of *Moscow Diary* in 1980 Scholem refers the reader to a letter Benjamin sent to Martin Buber shortly after his return. While insisting that the 'Moscow' text will be 'devoid of all theory', Benjamin speaks of his efforts to comprehend 'this new and disorienting language that loudly echoes through the acoustic mask of an entirely transformed environment' (Scholem and Adorno 1994: 313). He continues:

> I intend to present a picture of the city of Moscow as it is at this very moment. In this picture, 'all factuality is already theory' and therefore it refrains from any deductive abstraction, any prognostication, and, within certain bounds, even any judgment (Benjamin 1994: 313).

This method of pure description will be Benjamin's abiding approach to the AP for over a decade and, as such, subject to repeated criticism by Adorno and other key figures of the Frankfurt School in the latter half of the 1930s (see Wolin 1994: 163–212). It is clear, however, that this abstinence from explicit theorizing is viewed by Benjamin as a wholly justified manner of conveying the experience of the metropolitan environment. As will be elaborated on in later chapters, for Benjamin the built environment does not primarily register with its human inhabitants in cognitive or intellectual terms. Rather, *the modern city produces primarily physiological or somatic effects* and by this means induces changes in collective perception. Benjamin would only make such claims explicit in the writings of his final years, though there are many clues indicating that these convictions were arrived at in the crucial transitional period of the mid-1920s presently under consideration.

For Benjamin the built environment does not primarily register with its human inhabitants in cognitive or intellectual terms. Rather, *the modern city produces primarily physiological or somatic effects* and by this means induces changes in collective perception.

Just as Naples confronted Benjamin in terms of a strong contrast to Berlin, the first line of 'Moscow' speaks of learning 'to see Berlin through Moscow' (Benjamin 1999a: 22). The connection between image and experience is made immediately: 'What is true of the image of the city and its people applies also to the intellectual situation: a new optics is the most undoubted gain from a stay in Russia' (ibid.). The idea of a new optics is something Benjamin will pursue in celebrated essays and comments on photography and cinema in the 1930s. Already in 'Moscow', however, he indicates that the new metropolitan environment outstrips the visitor's perceptual capacities and calls for the supplementation of cinematic technology:

> Now the city turns into a labyrinth for the newcomer. ... The whole exciting sequence of topographical deceptions to which he falls prey could be shown only by a film: the city is on its guard against him, masks itself, flees, intrigues, lures him to wander its circles to the point of exhaustion (Benjamin 1999a: 24).

Within a week of his arrival in the city, Benjamin had taken the opportunity of viewing Sergei Eisenstein's *Battleship Potemkin* and Lev Kuleskov's *By the Law* (*Pozakonu*). Both directors were pioneering practitioners of cinematic montage, an artistic technique first introduced into the visual arts within cubism and subsequently developed in Dada and surrealism (see Vidler 2000: 99–122). After his return to Berlin Benjamin would write defending the politically tendentious nature of early Soviet cinema. Responding to contemporary German criticism of political bias, Benjamin remarked: 'The superiority of the Russian revolutionary film resides, just like the American comedy, in the very fact that both, in their own way, have taken a tendentious stance [*Tendenz*] as their basis to which they constantly and consistently return' (Benjamin 1991: 753; my translation). Such a comment makes it clear, at this relatively early point, that Benjamin had no objection to art being used for explicitly political ends. Legitimate politicization of art, however, is measured according to the degree that the message corresponds to the medium. It is primarily from this perspective that Benjamin defends early Soviet cinema. As he bluntly notes with respect to *Potemkin*'s glorification of the proletariat:

The proletariat is, however, the collective, just as these spaces [of the cinema] are spaces of the collective. And here, for the first time, film can complete that prismatic task that was begun with respect to the environment. *Potemkin* has had an epoch-making effect precisely because this was never before made so apparent. Here for the first time the movement of the masses has a thoroughly architectonic but not monumental character, which first justifies its cinematic recording (ibid.).

Here we find the first formulation of the theory of cinema spelt out in the mid-1930s in Benjamin's best-known essay, 'The Work of Art in the Age of Its Technological Reproducibility'. In the artwork essay, Benjamin describes cinematic technology as uniquely making possible 'a highly productive use of the human being's self-alienation' (Benjamin 2002: 113). Significantly, Benjamin sees in collective reception an important affinity between cinema and architecture (Benjamin 2002: 116). This common ground is hinted at in the defence of Russian cinema cited above, where Benjamin refers to its 'architectonic but not monumental character'. In the artwork essay a non-monumental architectonic mode of presentation calls for an altered mode of reception: 'Architecture has always offered the prototype of an artwork that is received in a state of distraction and through the collective. The laws of architecture's reception are highly instructive' (119–20). By this point (1935–6), Benjamin's approach to architecture has been mediated by influential and arguably decisive encounters with modernist architectural theory. While detailed consideration of these encounters will be tackled directly in Chapter 3, the connection made between metropolis and montage is worth pursuing immediately.

Architectural montage

In *Collage City* Colin Rowe and Fred Koetter identify two opposed currents in cultural modernism. The first, viewed as predominant in architecture, strives for 'unity, continuity, system', whereas the second embraces the method of collage and prizes 'irony, obliquity and multiple reference' (Koetter and Rowe 1984: 138). The method of collage (and by extension montage) they align with the notion *bricolage* or improvised construction, central to the work of the French anthropologist Claude Lévi-Strauss. While, they argue, 'the twentieth century architect had been the reverse of willing to think of himself as a "bricoleur" ' (139), they cite Le Corbusier as a significant counter-example:

> Indeed among architects only that great straddler Le Corbusier, sometimes hedgehog, sometimes fox, has displayed any sympathy towards this kind of thing. His buildings, though not his city plans, are loaded with the results of a process which might be considered more or less equivalent to that of collage. Objects and episodes are obtrusively imported and, while they retain the overtones of their source and origin, they also gain a wholly new impact from their changed context. In, for instance, the Ozenfant studio one is confronted with a mass of allusions and references which it would seem are all basically brought together by means of collage (140).

The disjunction observed here between Le Corbusier's design of individual domestic structures and his comprehensive urban designs is telling. For Benjamin, it was the arcade structure of the nineteenth century that prefigured the possibility of employing collage as a principle of urban design. It was not until cinema had reached a certain level of development, however, that this other modernism could really attain its progressive potential. As 'Moscow' makes clear, montage as a technique has the potential to bring together cinema and architecture in aesthetically and politically progressive ways. Benjamin was all too aware of regressive social forces intent on seeing only the crudely instrumental potential of modern techniques of construction. Such regressive appreciation would later offer significant support to the fascist tendency to naturalize technological development, that is, to view it as a tool for the direct mastery of organic and inorganic nature. One of the key virtues of montage as a technique, by contrast, is that it makes the denaturalized status of the artwork explicit by suspending any organic unity on the part of the producer or receiver. However, it is more readily apparent how this works in the case of the visual arts than in architecture. In the artwork essay Benjamin speaks of a twofold manner of architectural reception – tactile and optical. It is in the tactile mode that architecture can produce collective, largely unconscious habits:

Tactile reception comes about not so much by way of attention as by way of habit. The latter largely determines even the optical reception of architecture, which spontaneously takes the form of casual noticing, rather than attentive observation. Under certain circumstances, this form of reception shaped by architecture acquires canonical value. *For the tasks which face the human apparatus of perception at historical turning points cannot be performed solely by optical means – that is, by way of contemplation. They are mastered gradually – taking their cue from tactile reception – through habit* (Benjamin 2002: 120).

For Benjamin, it was the arcade structure of the nineteenth century that prefigured the possibility of employing collage as a principle of urban design.

The dominance of the tactile over the optical in architectural reception suggests a certain positioning of the receiver. As his defence of *Potemkin* makes clear, Benjamin sees cinematic montage as a technique uniquely suited to capturing the movement of the metropolitan population. Inspired by the work of the German sociologist Georg Simmel and his friend Sigfried Kracauer (later to become an influential film theorist), Benjamin grasped the collective mental state induced by the modern metropolis in terms of *distraction*. This notion is key to Benjamin's artwork essay and his mature art theory more generally (see Eiland 2005). It is important to note, however, that the German word translated as 'distraction' – *Zerstreuung* – carries more visceral, physiological connotations than the English term, and suggests a sense of violent dispersal. So understood, it can be more readily appreciated that Benjamin's notion of architectural reception relates not to those who produce architectural designs but rather to the metropolitan inhabitant.

Benjamin is in fact attempting to capture basic features of urban social dynamics in so far as the inhabitant is conditioned within the built environment, thereby developing historically specific sets of unreflective collective behaviour. From within the designer's studio such dynamics may appear as something to be ordered and controlled. A desire to resolve the contradictions and tensions produced by the metropolitan environment is much in evidence in modernist architectural theory and practice. The irony has often been noted that many of the most influential figures of architectural modernism experienced unease or even loathing in the face of actual cities. Benjamin, of course, did not think of himself as an architect or urban designer. But he did look at cities with the eye of a creative intellectual producer. From this perspective he was convinced that theory could no longer be produced according to the traditional model of dispassionate contemplation. If theory was to have any practical impact, he thought, it would have to correspond to profound changes in the everyday material environment made possible by industrial technology. In a word, Benjamin takes up his critical position in the midst of the dispersed and disorienting metropolitan labyrinth and resists the temptation to rise above this environment in pursuit of a commanding theoretical panorama.

Benjamin takes up his critical position in the midst of the dispersed and disorienting metropolitan labyrinth and resists the temptation to rise above this environment in pursuit of a commanding theoretical panorama.

In Moscow Benjamin feels he is in a place where a decisive encounter between modern technology and art is unfolding (see Curtis 2002: 201–15). While the final section of 'Moscow' concedes that, with the death of Lenin, the heroic period of Soviet Communism is over, Benjamin still views the crucial historical experiment as ongoing. In contrast to his bitter critique of the German metropolis, where he sees technology inevitably tied to conflict and war, in Moscow the 'revolutionary nature of true technology is emphasized ever more clearly' (Benjamin 1999a: 45). In the Soviet city the confrontation between urban modernity and more obviously natural elements of the built environment at the edges of the metropolis – which in Berlin presented such an apocalyptic landscape – offers traces of redemption:

> Nowhere does Moscow look like the city itself; at the most it resembles its outskirts. … The city is still interspersed with little wooden buildings in exactly the same Slavonic style as those found everywhere in the surroundings of Berlin. What looks so desolate in Brandenburg stone is attractive here, with the lovely colors of warm wood. … Longing [*Sehnsucht*] for Moscow is engendered not only by the snow, with its starry luster by night and its flowerlike crystals by day, but also by the sky. For between low roofs the horizon of the broad plains is constantly entering the city (Benjamin 1999a: 42; translation slightly modified).

While there are undertones of a nostalgic yearning for pre-modern simplicity in this passage, its dominant sense offers an alternative understanding of Benjamin's metropolitanism. Accordingly, it is the provisional nature of the built environment that attracts the writer: the fragility of wood instead of the permanence of stone. As the AP develops Benjamin will find the medium that suits his perspective best: glass (see Missac 1995: 147–72). Glass heightens the sense of impermanence in so far as its very materiality is perceptually tenuous. As Benjamin will come to express it in the 1930s, technological advances in the

As Benjamin will come to express it in the 1930s, technological advances in the use of glass herald new cities where individuals will no longer leave behind traces of their inhabitation. No other material could be better suited to explode the claustrophobia of the bourgeois interiors Benjamin experienced with a profound dread in his childhood.

use of glass herald new cities where individuals will no longer leave behind traces of their inhabitation. No other material could be better suited to explode the claustrophobia of the bourgeois interiors Benjamin experienced with a profound dread in his childhood. As he will express it in his 1929 essay on surrealism: 'To live in a glass house is a revolutionary virtue par excellence. It is also an intoxication, a moral exhibitionism, that we badly need' (Benjamin 1999a: 209). Benjamin had first dreamt of this intoxication of transparency as a young child in the loggia of his grandmother's Berlin apartment.

CHAPTER 2

Radicalism and Revolution

Benjamin and surrealism

An early entry in the 'Ancient Paris' section of the *Arcades Project* notes: 'The father of surrealism was Dada; its mother was an arcade' (Benjamin 1999b: 82). As is clear from his correspondence, from the summer of 1925 Benjamin was seriously engaged with surrealism and its early works (see Buck-Morss 1989: 253–75; Pensky 1993: 184–210). In a letter to Hugo von Hofmannsthal from 28 December he remarks: 'the more inclined I am to deal with some topical projects, especially the books by the Parisian surrealists, the more aware I become of the difficulty of finding a place somewhere for my ephemeral, although perhaps not superficial, considerations' (Scholem and Adorno 1994: 286). This connection between surrealism and a concern for the ephemeral is significant. As noted in the previous chapter, Benjamin's appreciation of the built environment involves an acute awareness of its transience. This awareness manifests itself in two quite distinct affective attitudes: melancholic nostalgia and euphoric intoxication. Benjamin aligns surrealism emphatically with the latter.

In his first published writing on surrealism (appearing in 1927 but most likely written in 1925), 'Dream Kitsch: Gloss on Surrealism', Benjamin introduces the theme of technological obsolescence early on:

> Technology consigns the outer image of things to a long farewell, like banknotes that are bound to lose their value. It is then that the hand retrieves this outer cast in dreams and, even as they are slipping away, makes contact with familiar contours. It catches hold of objects at their most threadbare and timeworn point. ... And which side does an object turn towards dreams? What point is its most decrepit? It is the side worn through by habit and patched with cheap maxims. The side which turns toward the dream is kitsch (Benjamin 1999a: 3).

From the early 1920s the group of friends that would be formally announced as the surrealist movement with André Breton's publication of the *Surrealist Manifesto* in 1924 had experimented with 'automatic writing'. Derived in part from Breton's knowledge of psychoanalytic techniques, automatic writing was revolutionary in so far as it sought to avoid self-censorship in artistic production. As far as possible such production was to express the spontaneous imaginative productions of the mind. For early surrealism this meant allowing the artist to produce in a suggestive state akin to daydreaming, where seemingly random associations would unfold without conscious effort to organize or rationalize material. Whereas Freudian psychoanalysis assumes such rational censorship to be indispensable to any viable psychic equilibrium, Breton insists that the work of the censor is grounded in a material social reality shot through with the mechanisms of what he terms 'absolute rationalism'. In the 1924 *Manifesto* Breton remarks:

> **Experience has found itself increasingly circumscribed. It paces back and forth in a cage from which it is more and more difficult to make it emerge. It too leans for support on what is most immediately expedient, and it is protected by the sentinels of common sense. Under the pretence of civilisation and progress, we have managed to banish from the mind everything that may rightly or wrongly be termed superstition or fancy; any kind of search for truth which is not in conformity with accepted practices is forbidden (Breton 1969: 10).**

What tends to undermine the recognition of surrealism as a revolutionary material practice is its identification of the imagination as the essential vehicle of social emancipation. When Breton remarks that the imagination 'is perhaps on the point of reasserting itelf, of reclaiming its rights' and further looks forward to the 'future resolution of … dream and reality, into a kind of absolute reality, a *surreality*' (ibid.), this readily suggests a kind of neo-Romanticism that calls for a retreat into comforting delusions in the face of a social environment increasing shaped by rigorously controlled material production.

In 'Dream Kitsch' Benjamin articulates a sense of surrealist method as historically situated. He refers to the 'ornament of conversation' that characterized the generation born around the middle of the nineteenth century, in other words the generation to which Benjamin's (and the surrealists') grandparents belonged. In the revolt against such ornament, surrealism turns to dream in order to retrieve the artist's childhood and so bring back into the present its world of nineteenth-century bourgeois interiors and decorative objects. The concern for historically situated objects makes clear the truly materialist perspective of the surrealists, who are 'less on the trail of the psyche than on the track of things' (Benjamin 1999a: 4). As will later be repeated in the extended essay 'Surrealism' published in 1929, recollecting the worn-out material culture of the nineteenth century ultimately has the purpose of appropriation, 'so as to take in the energies of an outlived world of things' (ibid.).

As we saw in the previous chapter, for Benjamin recollecting childhood is a key task connected to artistic development, in so far as the personal past is grasped as a promise for present existence. Understood in the broader context of a generation's relationship to cultural production, what Benjamin sees in surrealist method is an effort to redeem the transience of the modern material environment through the mediation of artistic methods of technological reproduction. The method of 'psychic automatism', cited by Breton in his 1924 definition of surrealism, points to a critical appropriation of the very mechanisms of mechanical reproduction made possible by advanced commodity capitalism (see Foster 1993: 157–91). Accordingly, Benjamin views surrealism through the lens of his own efforts in the mid-1920s to develop a theoretical method attuned to the broader productive means of his times.

What Benjamin sees in surrealist method is an effort to redeem the transience of the modern material environment through the mediation of artistic methods of technological reproduction.

From the late 1920s to the mid-1930s Breton led the Paris surrealists into an ever-closer alignment with revolutionary communism. In his lecture 'The Surrealist Situation of the Object', delivered in Prague in 1935, Breton indicates how he views the means employed and goals aimed at across a decade-and-a-half of surrealist practice:

> I for my part believe today in the possibility and the great interest of the experiment that consists in incorporating objects, ordinary or not, within a poem, or more exactly of composing a poem in which visual elements take their place between the words without ever duplicating them. ... To aid the systematic derangement of all the senses, a derangement recommended by Rimbaud and continuously made the order of the day by the Surrealists, it is my opinion that we must not hesitate to *bewilder sensation* ... (Breton 1969: 263).

It is clear from the context of this remark that Breton has in mind the method of montage. More specifically, he alludes to the juxtaposition of written and visual elements within a poetic composition, a combination that was typical for the surrealists in their joint and individual work. The art-historical background of the development of surrealist practice is crucially determined by the advent of photography. Breton explicitly recognized that this advent spelt the end for any aesthetic of mimetic realism. But rather than leading to the obsolescence of the poetic image he views photography as the means for its renewed deployment. The key point here is that the production of the poetic image can no longer be consigned to a specific practice that might be labelled 'aesthetic' in contrast to the 'mechanical' processes of photography. Rather, objects produced according to surrealist methods are understood to manifest the collective utopianism or 'dream-life' of the machines of photographic reproduction themselves. Such utopianism points to potentially redemptive collective practices made possible by use of the technological means of production themselves. Benjamin also picks up on the political potential of bringing together word and image through the technique of montage in his 1934 essay 'The Author as Producer':

> What we require of the photographer is the ability to give his picture a caption that wrenches it from modish commerce and gives it a revolutionary

use value. But we will make this demand most emphatically when we – the writers – take up photography. Here, too, therefore, technical progress is for the author as producer the foundation of his political progress. In other words, only by transcending the specialization in the process of intellectual production – a specialization that, in the bourgeois view, constitutes its order – can one make this production politically useful (Benjamin 1999a: 775).

Breton's way of expressing this process around the same time is to speak of the 'bewildering of the senses' as possessing a revolutionary tendency. In the 'Political Position of Today's Art', a further lecture given in Prague in the spring of 1935, Breton elaborates on the political significance of surrealist practice. He spells out how the method of psychic automatism taken to define surrealism in the 1924 *Manifesto* did not in fact signify a retreat into individual aesthetic consciousness. It was rather a question of devising artistic practices that would facilitate a breaking free from the very mechanisms that materially isolate individuals under social conditions subject to intensive technological mediation. In Breton's words:

Psychic automatism ... has never constituted an end in itself for surrealism, and to claim the contrary is to show bad faith. The premeditated energy in poetry and in art ... necessarily had some day to discover the immense reservoir from which symbols spring fully armed and spread to collective life through the work of a few men. It was a question of foiling, foiling forever, the coalition of forces that seek to make the unconscious incapable of any sort of violent irruption (Breton 1969: 231–2).

Benjamin's struggle to articulate the political significance of the AP in the mid-1930s similarly relates to the effort to find the point at which artistic production can be plausibly revolutionary in nature. In a summary sketch of the AP from 1935 – bearing the title 'Paris, the Capital of the Nineteenth Century' – Benjamin has recourse to the idea of a collective image-consciousness:

Corresponding to the form of the new means of production, which in the beginning is still ruled by the form of the old (Marx), are images in the collective consciousness in which the new is permeated with the old. These images are wish images; in them the collective seeks both to overcome and to transfigure the immaturity of the social product and the inadequacies in the social organization of production (Benjamin 2002: 33).

Here Benjamin vacillates between notions of collective consciousness and a collective *unconscious*. To the latter he ascribes images that envisage the future in terms of a state of harmonious redemption akin to the classless society Marx thought would result from the revolutionary praxis of the proletariat: 'In the dream in which each epoch entertains images of its successor, the latter appears wedded to elements of primal history [*Urgeschichte*] – that is, to elements of a classless society' (33–4). Around the same time Breton similarly connects surrealist practice with images signifying a dream-reality that can be made collectively conscious and so emancipating: 'These perceptions, through their very tendency to assert themselves as objective perceptions, are of such a nature as to be bewildering and revolutionary, in the sense that they urgently call for something to answer them in outer reality' (Breton 1969: 278). The image as carrier of revolutionary, utopian desire thus constitutes a crucial element of common ground in the respective conceptions of artistic production put forward by Benjamin and Breton.

The image as carrier of revolutionary, utopian desire thus constitutes a crucial element of common ground in the respective conceptions of artistic production put forward by Benjamin and Breton.

The *Arcades Project* and modern architecture

Whereas surrealism was born through the death of its Dadaist father, its mother – the arcade – survived its inception. Indeed, through Benjamin's work on the Paris arcades we might even say that the mother has enjoyed a second life.

While the AP maintained an almost mythical standing in the decades following Benjamin's death in 1940, intensive research done since its first publication in German in 1982 has since given it canonical status. However, the original title given to the project – *Passagen-Werk* – indicates that this 'work' cannot easily be looked upon as the author's *magnum opus*. Adorno, to whom the task of organizing the materials relating to the AP originally fell, came to the decision that only Benjamin himself would have been in a position to prepare it for publication. The editor who eventually summoned up the courage to bring the AP to the public, Rolf Tiedemann, has recourse to an architectural analogy:

> The fragments of the *Passagen-Werk* can be compared to the materials used in building a house, the outline of which has just been marked in the ground or whose foundations are just being dug. ... The five or six sections of each exposé should have corresponded to the same number of chapters in the book or, to continue the analogy, to the five or six floors of the projected house. Next to the foundations we find the neatly piled excerpts, which would have been used to construct the walls; Benjamin's own thoughts would have provided the mortar to hold the building together. ... Once familiar with the architecture of the whole, the reader will be able to read the excerpts without great difficulty and pinpoint in almost every one that element which must have fascinated Benjamin (Benjamin 1999b: 931).

Against the notion of a house plan with its materials of construction carefully laid out around the site, it is perhaps more credible to propose Benjamin's own preferred structure – the labyrinth. As shown, already in the opening section of *One-Way Street* Benjamin had protested against 'the pretentious, universal gesture of the book' (Benjamin 1996: 444). Tiedemann's analogy recalls the title of another early section of that work, the 'Manorially Furnished Ten-Room Apartment', with its sinister and claustrophobic bourgeois interior. Accordingly, the comparison of the AP to an architectural drawing or plan is problematic on a number of levels.

It is doubtful whether Benjamin was striving for anything like comprehensive or holistic understanding, either on his part or that of his prospective reader. The method of the project is self-consciously fragmentary and allusive in nature, rather than cumulative and deductive. While the sketches or exposés of the AP identify material-historical leitmotifs, these function as ways into the maze rather than as floor plans. As in first encounters with a built environment, Benjamin's approach emphasizes the singularity of his materials and avoids the typical theoretical tendency of assimilating them by means of a static, systematic perspective. Thus, the project is intentionally not provided with any 'architecture of the whole'. In light of Benjamin's underlying attitude to the nineteenth-century bourgeois interior, it is important to view the AP as similarly motivated by a desire to explode an illusory understanding of space that is also operative within traditional, as opposed to genuinely critical, theory. In fact, as we shall see, the last decade-and-a-half of Benjamin's work is driven by the conviction that theory should learn to live without the comprehensive conceptual plan, just as modern humanity was giving up the need to dwell in the sense of leaving personal traces in its immediate material environment. The point was to take leave of the contemplative attitude in construction, not with nostalgic regret but with something akin to revolutionary passion.

The question remains: why *did* Benjamin devote so much intellectual effort to a project centred on the nineteenth-century Paris arcades? While it is relatively

Benjamin's work is driven by the conviction that theory should learn to live without the comprehensive conceptual plan, just as modern humanity was giving up the need to dwell in the sense of leaving personal traces in its immediate material environment. The point was to take leave of the contemplative attitude in construction, not with nostalgic regret but with something akin to revolutionary passion.

easy to assemble various recorded sources that informed Benjamin's approach to the arcades, the decision on the theme itself remains puzzling. An initial clue can be gleaned from the very fact that the arcades had never been accorded canonical status as an architectural type. In his exhaustive account of the arcade as an architectural structure, Johann Friedrich Geist underscores the unofficial nature of its inception and development:

> The arcade was never an object of instruction. It was never chosen as the theme for the Prix de Rôme. It cannot be found in contemporary textbooks as an architectural exercise. The architectural concept of the arcade is promulgated anonymously, through travelogues, word-of-mouth reports, direct observation, and study of the arcade site itself. It is difficult to reconstruct an unambiguously demonstrable course of development of the arcade through the [nineteenth] century. We lack, especially for the first stages, records, names of architects, building plans, and any statement of the builders concerning their motives (Geist 1985: 64).

Benjamin grasped this official architectural obscurity of the origins of the modern arcade in light of Sigfried Giedion's idea, that 'whenever the nineteenth century feels itself to be unobserved, it grows bold' (Benjamin 1999b: 154). This idea is expressed in *Bauen in Frankreich* (*Building in France*), published by Giedion in 1928 and read avidly at the time by Benjamin. Through this work more than any other Benjamin came to appreciate the revolutionary potential of modernist architecture. At the time of the book's publication Giedion held the position of the first secretary of the Congrès Internationale d'Architecture Moderne (CIAM). Giedion's written work was a impassioned attempt to demonstrate that the modern spirit of construction could in fact be traced back to developments beginning 100 years before:

> *The 'new' architecture had its origins at the moment of industrial formation around 1830*, at the moment of the transformation from hand work to industrial production. We scarcely have the right to compare our century with the nineteenth as far as the boldness of its advance and its works are concerned (Giedion 1995: 86).

While Le Corbusier's *Towards an Architecture* from 1923 stressed the spiritual vocation of the architect, Giedion's account inflects the relationship between engineer and architect differently, in a manner that was bound to catch Benjamin's attention:

> Unconsciously, the *constructor* assumes the role of a guardian in the nineteenth century: by continuously pressing new means upon the architect, he keeps the latter from altogether losing himself in a vacuum. *The constructor presses for a design that is both anonymous and collective.* He renounces the architect's artistic bombast. Upsets his position. That is his function (Giedion 1995: 94).

Benjamin, who in the late 1920s and early 1930s was attempting to articulate how the social function of the artist changes once the artwork is placed in the service of the proletariat rather than bourgeois consumer, would have been drawn to this idea of anonymous, collective construction. Early in 1929, while working on his essay 'Surrealism', Benjamin wrote to Giedion expressing the excitement he had felt reading *Building in France*:

> As I read through your book ... I am struck by the heart-quickening difference between a radical attitude and radical knowing. What you exemplify is the latter, and therefore you are capable of highlighting tradition – or rather, discovering it – within the present day (Benjamin 1999a: 832).

An adequate grasp of the revolutionary potential of modern architecture – and, by implication, of the nineteenth-century arcades – is thus for Benjamin a question of 'radical knowledge'. As we saw in the previous chapter, such knowledge is intimately connected to Benjamin's efforts to develop a new method of theoretical construction analogous to montage in the visual arts and cinema. Clearly, the connection between Benjamin's methodology and his focus on the arcades requires further elucidation.

In the section of the AP concerned with theory of knowledge, Benjamin again cites Giedion's appreciation of the development of modern architecture as key

An adequate grasp of the revolutionary potential of modern
architecture – and, by implication, of the nineteenth-century
arcades – is thus for Benjamin a question of 'radical
knowledge'.

to his own philosophy of history. In the following comment he makes a direct
connection between the revolutionary intention of his own theoretical practice
and a crucial intertwining of surrealist practice and modern architectural
construction:

> [The interior décor of the nineteenth-century is] material of vital importance
> politically; this is demonstrated by the attraction of the surrealists to these
> things. In other words: just as Giedion teaches us to read off the basic
> features of today's architecture in the buildings around 1850, we, in turn,
> would recognize today's life, today's forms, in the life of the apparently
> secondary, lost forms of that epoch (Benjamin 1999b: 458).

In conjunction with Giedion's further idea that 'in the nineteenth-century
construction plays the role of the subconscious' (Benjamin 1999b: 391, 858),
Benjamin's train of thought becomes apparent: just as modernist architecture
converts the previous century's unconscious principles of construction into a

Just as modernist architecture converts the previous century's
unconscious principles of construction into a conscious
historical task, so surrealism reveals the revolutionary potential
of nineteenth-century bourgeois material culture.

conscious historical task, so surrealism reveals the revolutionary potential of nineteenth-century bourgeois material culture. While the explicit focus of *Building in France* is nineteenth-century industrial construction (bridges, railway stations and factories), Benjamin focuses on the place privileged by the surrealists, the arcades.

Beyond his reading of Aragon's *Paris Peasant* – alluded to in Benjamin's correspondence and notes from the AP – the various sketches and introductions to the AP offer important clues as to the reasons for Benjamin's choice of the Paris arcades. Arguably the most compelling relates to the rapid decline of the arcades from the height of fashion to eerie obsolescence within a generation or two. Following Marx's analysis of the commodity as an object of collective fetishism, Benjamin sees the arcade as the pre-eminent space of commodity consumption at the unique historical moment when the production of luxury items is organized on an industrial scale. From more modest beginnings in the first third of the nineteenth century, by mid-century improved constructive techniques in iron and glass allowed the arcades to assume massive proportions in housing the unparalleled commodity displays of the world exhibitions. In the 1935 version of the text 'Paris, the Capital of the Nineteenth Century', Benjamin invokes the theory of distraction, first developed in relation to cinema, to express the mode of perception involved in the mass consumption of the commodity:

> [The world exhibitions] open a phantasmagoria which a person enters in order to be distracted. The entertainment industry makes this easier by elevating the person to the level of commodity. He surrenders to its manipulations while enjoying this alienation from himself and others (Benjamin 2002: 37).

Benjamin thus selected the arcades in virtue of their function as the original spaces of industrially produced commodity consumption. The basic Marxian thesis regarding the commodity is that it transforms real relations between persons into apparent relations between things. Benjamin's supplement to this thesis involves excavating the material context in which this transformation in mass perception could first occur. An analogical process of reasoning thus becomes apparent: as the artist relates to images of his childhood, so the political theorist relates to the original places of modern alienation. In both cases the task is not straightforwardly one of overcoming the past in so far as it survives within current material culture. It is rather a question of redeeming utopian traces within what is taken to be a profoundly alienated or 'accursed' environment.

The AP was, according to Benjamin's characterization, concerned with the 'primal history [*Urgeschichte*] of the nineteenth century' (Benjamin 2002: 52). The operation of historical recollection is, as we have seen, intrinsic to Benjamin's methodology. The arcades became the focus of his mature work as they were, in his estimation, the place where modern modes of alienated mass perception came into existence in a particularly intensive and comprehensive manner. The radicalism of Benjamin's theoretical practice, therefore, resides in his effort *to trace the social pathologies of the twentieth century back to their early nineteenth-century roots*. Only by doing this, Benjamin thought, could there be any hope of retrieving the utopian promise of the very powers and processes that gave rise to the accursed spaces of modern consumption.

The arcades became the focus of his mature work as they were, in his estimation, the place where modern modes of alienated mass perception came into existence in a particularly intensive and comprehensive manner. The radicalism of Benjamin's theoretical practice, therefore, resides in his effort *to trace the social pathologies of the twentieth century back to their early nineteenth-century roots.*

The dialectic of technology and nature

As the recently published collection of essays *Walter Benjamin and* The Arcades
Project demonstrates, contemporary approaches to Benjamin's work are
characterized by their variety and eclecticism. Given Benjamin's repudiation of
theoretical specialization, the profusion of interpretive perspectives applied to
his work may be regarded as appropriate and useful. While attempts to
reconstruct a comprehensive plan for the fragmentary AP may be in vain, this
does not mean, however, that it lacks unity of intent. Such unity, however, is
not to be sought within the collected materials of the project themselves. It is
rather a function of Benjamin's political stance, something that he was able to
clarify most effectively through his close personal relationship with Bertold
Brecht.

Benjamin first came to know Brecht in 1929 through Lacis when she was
working as Brecht's assistant. Throughout the crucial period of the early 1930s,
with the political atmosphere of Europe rapidly darkening, Benjamin spent much
time in Brecht's company and came to appreciate in practical terms what art in
the service of the proletariat could mean. As with all of Benjamin's key personal
encounters, his relationship with Brecht allowed him to clarify and refine
experiences and ideas he had articulated years before (see Wolin 1994: 139–61).
Nevertheless, such a refinement process was profound and long-lasting in the
case of his response to Brecht. In theoretical terms the key result of this
response was a radical recasting of the relationship between technology and
nature. This reflected, in turn, back on Benjamin's understanding of how artistic
practice could assume a politically revolutionary character. Benjamin's
articulation of the four-way relationship between art and politics, technology
and nature constitutes a further aspect of the radicalism of his thinking.

Diary entries for May and June 1931 give an impression of Benjamin's initial
reaction to Brecht's ideas. Of pivotal significance to Benjamin's appreciation of
modern architecture is his response to the refrain of the first poem in Brecht's
collection, *Lesebuch für Städtebewohner* (*Reader for Citydwellers*) – 'erase the
traces'. Here Benjamin formulates an insight to which he will often return in the

following years, an insight which plays a crucial role in the account of Benjamin's appreciation of architecture offered in this book:

> What is possible among the pieces of furniture of the Bauhaus is no more than a bare lodging [*ein Hausen*] when compared with life in a bourgeois dwelling [*Wohnen*], whose interior compels the inhabitant to adopt a maximum number of habits. ... The modern style of building, whatever else may be said of it, has now created rooms in which it is hard to leave such traces (this is why glass and metal have become so important) and which make it almost impossible to acquire habits in the first place. This is why the rooms are empty and often adjustable at will (Benjamin 1999a: 472–3).

This opposition between dwelling (in German, *wohnen*) and mere lodging or housing (*hausen*) will become crucial for the section of the AP dealing with the nineteenth-century bourgeois interior. While more detailed analysis of this theme will be offered in the following chapter, it is also directly relevant to the present question of Benjamin's understanding of the nature–technology relationship. Benjamin offers a radical interpretation of modern technology, in so far as he ascribes to it a power to reshape human nature not merely superficially but profoundly, from the base up. This does not mean, however, that he adopts a position of straightforward environmental determinism. After all, while technology necessarily involves material mechanisms and effects, it is also itself the effect of human transformation of the natural environment. Put simply, Benjamin's understanding is dialectical, in the sense that environment and social structure are *mutually* determining. As we saw in the previous chapter, Benjamin understands material culture as always carrying a historical index. This index bears two faces: a *catastrophic* aspect that looks back at the

Benjamin offers a radical interpretation of modern technology, in so far as he ascribes to it a power to reshape human nature not merely superficially but profoundly, from the base up.

ruins of the past, and a *utopian* aspect that indicates the possibility of redemption in the present.

Taking a step back to *One-Way Street* provides an opportunity for further clarification of Benjamin's understanding of the nature–technology relation. The final section of that text, 'To the Planetarium', reflects on the massive deployment of modern technology to destructive ends during the events of the First World War. Even in the shadow of the horror of those events, which had traumatized so many of his generation, Benjamin sees the possibility of a redemptive transformation. He expresses this possibility through an enigmatic analogy:

> The mastery of nature (so the imperialists teach) is the purpose of all technology. But who would trust a cane wielder who proclaimed the mastery of children by adults to be the purpose of education? Is not education, above all, the indispensable ordering of the relationship between generations and therefore mastery (if we are to use this term) of that relationship and not of children? And likewise technology is mastery not of nature but of the relation between nature and man (Benjamin 1996: 487).

The task of the poetic image, as we have seen, it to retrieve utopian traces from a childhood environment. For Benjamin the environment in question was the nineteenth-century bourgeois interior of his parents and grandparents. As he relates in his writings on Berlin, his childhood world protected him from exposure to the misery of the working class. When he first came to explore working-class districts of Berlin as a young man it was through encounters with the city's prostitutes (Benjamin 2002: 404–5). In the AP Benjamin lays particular stress on the idea of the prostitute as an emblem of the most intense and pervasive commodity fetishism and alienation. He expresses this thought in extremely condensed fashion in 'Paris, the Capital of the Nineteenth Century', where he speaks of the prostitute in terms of an object of consumption combining 'seller and sold in one' (Benjamin 2002: 40).

Emblematically, the prostitute represents the intensified and proliferated alienation of the nineteenth-century working class under the conditions of modern production (see Buck-Morss 2006). These conditions were in large part brought about through technological advances that made mechanized mass manufacturing possible. Whereas the bourgeois ('imperialist') perspective grasps technology as a means to master nature, for the working class in the nineteenth century industrial technology in fact signified the reconfiguration of their workplace and working habits, and thence of their very 'nature'. In this light, 'mastery of nature' is actually class oppression. While it might be supposed that technological advances must always work to further the dominant social class, Benjamin's reflection in 'To the Planetarium' envisages a quite different possibility of social reconciliation. But this possibility is grasped as anything but historically inevitable:

> Men [*Menschen*] as a species completed their development thousands of years ago; but mankind [*Menschheit*] as a species is just beginning. For mankind a new *physis* is being organized in technology. In this new nature mankind's contact with the cosmos develops differently than in peoples and families. ... The paroxysm of genuine cosmic experience is not tied to that tiny fragment of nature that we are accustomed to call 'Nature.' In the nights of annihilation of the last war, the structure of mankind [*Gliederbau der Menschheit*] was shaken by a feeling that resembled the bliss of the epileptic. And the revolts that followed it were the first attempt of mankind to bring the new body under control. The power of the proletariat is the measure of its convalescence (Benjamin 1996: 487; translation slightly modified).

This description of the relationship between modern technology and nature points to the same polarity of catastrophic reality and utopian potentiality that was shown to characterize Benjamin's understanding of nineteenth-century material culture. It would be a mistake to view this polarity as indicative of uncertainty or ambivalence on Benjamin's part. He is not merely expressing the banal truism that technology can be used for good or evil ends. His point is rather that technology cannot be adequately grasped as a means for human ends without considering how human nature is fundamentally changed by those very means. In this way Benjamin anticipates the idea, popularized by Marshall McLuhan in the 1960s, that technological media of production and reproduction bring about reconfigurations or 'extensions' of the human body and its social image. The question concerning the utopian potentialities of modern technology is not, for Benjamin, something technological in nature. It is a question of political practice.

Benjamin anticipates the idea, popularized by Marshall McLuhan in the 1960s, that technological media of production and reproduction bring about reconfigurations or 'extensions' of the human body and its social image.

Regressive and progressive reactions to modern technology

It is useful to compare Benjamin's understanding of technology with that worked out around the same time by his German philosophical contemporary, Martin Heidegger (see Hannsen 2005). Given the sustained interest in Heidegger's work within architectural practice and theory in recent decades (see Frampton 1995; Harries 1998; Sharr 2007), this comparison is particularly relevant. There are many noteworthy biographical points of contact between Benjamin and Heidegger. They were both students of the neo-Kantian philosopher Heinrich Rickert at the University of Freiburg in Germany. Benjamin studied at Freiburg in 1913 while Heidegger was working on his *Habilitation* concerned with the scholastic thinker Duns Scotus. Both men were attracted to the German and Austrian poetry of the early twentieth century. In Heidegger's case the work of Georg Trakl (who was financially supported in part by the young Ludwig Wittgenstein) held particular attraction. For Benjamin it was the slightly older generation of Austrian poets, which included such figures as Stefan George, Hugo von Hofmannsthal and Karl Kraus. Both thinkers held Rilke's work in high esteem. However, these common reference points simply serve to make the divergence of their mature thinking all the more noteworthy. Most significant for the present context is the stark opposition between Benjamin's visceral metropolitanism and Heidegger's unwavering provincialism.

Heidegger's text 'Building, Dwelling, Thinking' from 1951 is often taken as central in discussions of his understanding of technology, space and architecture. The fact that Heidegger begins this text by warning the reader that his reflections have nothing to say about the practicalities of building and architectural design has not prevented commentators from drawing out such a connection at great length. The concern in the present context is not to question such efforts of interpretation and application, but rather to bring Benjamin's position into sharper focus against the foil of Heidegger's stance. In typical fashion Heidegger begins 'Building, Dwelling, Thinking' by questioning the seemingly unproblematic idea that in order to dwell we must build. Through extensive passages on the etymological roots of the German term for building, *Bauen*, Heidegger arrives at the conclusion that 'building' in fact means 'to be' and that 'building is really dwelling'. Thus, against the idea that we build in order to dwell, Heidegger asserts that dwelling in fact makes building possible. In a highly evocative passage Heidegger brings together the various threads of his essay:

> *Only if we are capable of dwelling, only then can we build.* Let us think for a while of a farmhouse in the Black Forest, which was built some two hundred years ago by the dwelling of peasants. Here the self-sufficiency of the power to let earth and heaven, divinities and mortals enter *in simple oneness* into things, ordered the house. It placed the farm on the wind-sheltered mountain slope looking south, among the meadows close to the spring. It gave it the wide overhanging shingle roof whose proper slope bears up under the burden of snow, and which, reaching deep down, shields the chambers against the storms of the long winter nights. It did not forget the altar corner behind the community table; it made room in its chamber for the hallowed places of childbed and the 'tree of the dead' – for that is what they call a coffin there: the *Totenbaum* – and in this way it designed for the different generations under one roof the character of their journey through time. A craft which, itself sprung from dwelling, still uses its tools and frames as things, built the farmhouse (Heidegger 2008: 361–2).

Similar passages can also be found in 'The Origin of the Work of Art', the original text of which is drawn from a series of lectures Heidegger gave in 1935 and 1936 (thus coinciding with Benjamin's own essay on the artwork). In his artwork essay Heidegger passes over in silence the radical changes in artistic representation introduced by various avant-garde movements in the early twentieth century. Similarly, in the passage above, Heidegger chooses a pre-industrial Black Forest farmhouse as exemplary and accentuates the natural setting of the structure. The description clearly offers an image of the dwelling place that emphasizes the harmonious, almost timeless unity of the artificial and the natural. Just as his analysis of the artwork from the mid-1930s brackets out the central focus of Benjamin's contemporaneous essay (technologies of reproduction), Heidegger's account of dwelling pointedly ignores the revolution in construction ushered in by the proponents of modernist architecture in the 1920s and 1930s.

Despite the fact that Heidegger's chief work – *Being and Time* from 1927 – turned on the rejection of all essentialist notions of human nature within the western tradition of thought, his later account of dwelling takes little if any account of modern historical conditions. As a result his thoughts on dwelling arguably have little to contribute to our understanding of the impact of technology and architecture on modern society. The development of Benjamin's thinking, by stark contrast, is profoundly shaped by his efforts to understand the dialectic of technology and nature by way of an analysis of the transformation of social organization through modern means of production. This, at least, was the way Benjamin saw the key difference between his own approach and that of Heidegger. In a letter to Scholem, Benjamin makes the following remark, in connection with his need to grasp Marx's theory of material history as an underpinning for the analyses of the AP: 'This is where I will find Heidegger, and I expect sparks will fly from the shock of the confrontation between our two very different ways of looking at history' (Scholem and Adorno 1994: 359–60). Benjamin elaborates on his point within the section of the AP devoted to history and material culture:

> The new historical thinking that, in general and in particular, is characterized
> by higher concreteness, redemption of periods of decline, revision of
> periodization, presently stands as such a point, and its utilization in a

reactionary or a revolutionary sense is now being decided. In this regard, the writings of the Surrealists and the new book by Heidegger [*Being and Time*, published in 1927] point to one and the same crisis in its two possible solutions (Benjamin 1999b: 544–5).

It is clear that here Heidegger falls on the side of reaction and surrealism that of revolution. In 'The Author as Producer' – Benjamin marks out – in a manner directly opposed to the nostalgic-regressive stance of Heidegger – a way towards a politically progressive understanding and use of modern art. Here he explicitly aligns himself with Brecht's notion of functional transformation (*Umfunktionierung*). Benjamin's call for writers to take up photography and so bring images into theory has already been mentioned. This exhortation is motivated by the conviction that advances in technology have radically modified the role of the artist as a specialized producer. Just as the practice of montage allowed 'accursed' everyday material culture to enter the 'sacred' sphere of high art, so in general must the modern artistic producer appropriate the modern means of technological production. Returning to a passage cited earlier, Benjamin continues:

In 'The Author as Producer' Benjamin marks out – in a manner directly opposed to the nostalgic-regressive stance of Heidegger – a way towards a politically progressive understanding and use of modern art.

Here, too, therefore, technical progress is for the author as producer the foundation of his political progress. In other words, only by transcending the specialization in the process of intellectual production – a specialization that, in the bourgeois view, constitutes its order – can one make this production politically useful. ... The author as producer discovers – even as he discovers his solidarity with the proletariat – his solidarity with certain other producers who earlier seemed scarcely to concern him (Benjamin 1999a: 775).

This sense of the artist's solidarity with the working class is further clarified through Benjamin's comments on cinema in the artwork essay. Here the socially revolutionary potentialities of cinema that Benjamin had first pondered in the wake of his visit to Moscow are drawn out in greater detail. Speaking of the way in which modern cinema achieves 'the most intensive interpenetration of reality with equipment' (Benjamin 2002: 116), Benjamin observes that 'the same public which reacts progressively to a slapstick comedy inevitably displays a backward reaction toward surrealism' (117). Just as 'To the Planetarium' opposed the use of technology in modern warfare to a possible alignment with a new *physis* of humanity, so in the artwork essay Benjamin looks to the modern medium of cinema with a view to its socially and politically progressive potential:

> *The most important social function of film is to establish equilibrium between human beings and the apparatus.* Film achieves this goal not only in terms of man's representation of himself to the camera but also in terms of his representation of his environment by means of this apparatus. On the one hand, film furthers insight into the necessities governing our lives by its use of close-ups, by its accentuation of hidden details in familiar objects, and by its exploration of commonplace milieux through the ingenious guidance of the camera; on the other hand, it manages to assure us of a vast and unsuspected field of action [*Spielraum*] (Benjamin 2002: 117).

In the previous chapter we encountered Benjamin's idea that the modern metropolis could be more readily assimilated through cinematic montage. It was also noted how Benjamin highlights collective reception as a key feature common to architecture and film. Finally, Benjamin's notion of 'distraction' and Breton's idea of perceptual 'bewilderment' propose the common task of bringing society to adopt a mode of reception suited to the modern environment. When Benjamin writes about 'establishing equilibrium between human beings and the apparatus' by means of cinema, this readily evokes the idea of collective alienation through technological conditioning. As the rest of the passage makes clear, however, the underlying idea is that modern technology can work to bring human perception into an accord with the material environment. This indicates that, for Benjamin, modern technology is the crucial mediating term in the dialectical relation between human society and its material environment. Accordingly, *the revolutionary radicalism of Benjamin's thinking resides in the idea that certain practices of cultural production can progressively align artistic construction with the cause of collective emancipation.*

The revolutionary radicalism of Benjamin's thinking resides in the idea that certain practices of cultural production can progressively align artistic construction with the cause of collective emancipation.

Architectural modernism and the politics of form

Stepping back from Benjamin's complex technological utopianism and viewing it in light of the profound disenchantment with modernism that became widespread from the 1960s on, the contemporary resonance and relevance of Benjamin's perspective may at first appear doubtful. In *Architecture and Utopia* (first published in Italian in 1973) the architectural historian and theorist Manfredo Tafuri contends that architectural modernism should be understood as having offered merely formal solutions to material economic and political problems of the time:

> beginning in the fourth decade of the nineteenth-century, realistic utopianism and utopian realism overlap and complement each other. The decline of the social utopia sanctioned ideology's surrender to the *politics of things* brought about by the laws of profit. Architectural, artistic and urban ideology was left with the *utopia of form* as a way of recovering the human totality through an ideal synthesis, as a way of embracing disorder through order (Tafuri 1976: 47–8).

'Utopia of form' is, for Tafuri, socially and politically regressive and remains fundamental to the cultural avant-garde in the first third of the twentieth century. Drawing repeatedly on Benjamin's thought relating to Charles Baudelaire and Georg Simmel's analysis of the modern metropolis as an environment of intensive psychological shock, in an earlier sketch of his work Tafuri insists that form and plan were modernist architecture's compensatory response to the modern city. Form is understood by architectural modernism as something capable of transforming urban chaos into order. Through the ideology of form Tafuri sees modernist architecture and urbanism as intervening to convert aspirations of earlier avant-garde movements into material reality:

> **It was at this point that architecture was able to enter the scene, by absorbing and overcoming all the demands of the historic avant-garde – and indeed by throwing them into crisis, since architecture alone was in a position to provide answers to the demands made by Cubism, Futurism, Dada, De Stijl, and all the various Constructivisms and Productivisms (Tafuri 1998: 20).**

In reality, however, this apparent overcoming amounted to realizing avant-garde utopianism as an ideology of *design* 'inherent in [productive] activity itself' (ibid.). In this way, modernist architecture absorbs and focuses the emancipatory, utopian aspirations of the artistic avant-garde and meshes them with the realism of material construction. Whatever the merits of Tafuri's critique of modern architecture, it is clear that the political radicalism of Benjamin's conception of art takes another path. As shown in the previous chapter, Benjamin's radical and abiding concern relates to the politically progressive potential of artistic production.

While Benjamin's writings display a remarkable sensitivity to the built environment, his experience of this environment is always held in a dynamic tension between actual catastrophe and potential redemption. He clearly found traces of the latter in the use of modern building materials such as iron and glass. As shown, however, Benjamin does not share the environmental determinism that is typical of architectural modernism. There is little explicitly stated in Benjamin's writings – beyond his enthusiasm for Giedion – to suggest an intimate or privileged relationship between his idea of progressive artistic production and modernist architecture as such. That privilege is clearly accorded to photography and, more obviously, cinema. And yet Benjamin's understanding of the radical connections between art and nature, technology and society undoubtedly does open up fruitful paths for architectural theory and practice. Some of these paths can be explored through further consideration of Benjamin's analysis of modernism.

CHAPTER 3

Modernism and Memory

Modernity and modernism

The previous two chapters have sketched the contours of Benjamin's experience of the built environment and his appreciation of the need to revolutionize theoretical method in line with modern productive and aesthetic practice. The central theme of this chapter is Benjamin's appreciation of modernity and, more specifically, modernism as it expressed itself in art and architecture in the nineteenth and early twentieth centuries. While Benjamin embraced the pioneering spirit evident in modernist architecture in the early decades of the twentieth century, he was at best ambivalent towards its rhetoric of triumphant progressivism. To temper this rhetoric Benjamin follows Giedion's lead in tracing modernism back to the mid-nineteenth century. In this context Benjamin's intensive study of Charles Baudelaire was to provide the main contours for reconstructing what he called 'the primal history of nineteenth century'.

> While Benjamin embraced the pioneering spirit evident in modernist architecture in the early decades of the twentieth century, he was at best ambivalent towards its rhetoric of triumphant progressivism.

The description of modernity offered by Baudelaire in his 1863 essay 'The Painter of Modern Life' has become canonical and offers a useful starting point for addressing the more specific theme of modernism: 'By "modernity" I mean the ephemeral, the fugitive, the contingent, the half of art whose other half is the eternal and the immutable' (Baudelaire 1964: 13). The experience of transience appears to stand at the heart of many of Benjamin's texts. At the beginning of Chapter 1 this was shown to characterize at a deep level Benjamin's appreciation of the physical environment of his childhood. Rather than capturing the fragility of the built environment in a predominantly elegiac and nostalgic register, however, Benjamin's writings in the 1930s always attempt to identify positive, socially transformative potential present within the very process of decay itself. Like many of his contemporaries, Benjamin accepts that the material conditions of advanced technological production are marked by historical, social rupture. In a recent work, bearing a title – *Paris, Capital of Modernity* – that consciously echoes the one Benjamin gave to his sketch of the *Arcades Project*, David Harvey begins by taking up the common idea of modernity as historical discontinuity:

> One of the myths of modernity is that it constitutes a radical break with the past. The break is supposedly of such an order as to make it possible to see the world as a tabula rasa, upon which the new can be inscribed without reference to the past – or, if the past gets in the way, through its obliteration ... I call this idea of modernity a myth because the notion of a radical break has a certain persuasive and pervasive power in the face of abundant evidence that it does not, and cannot, possibly occur (Harvey 2003: 1).

Benjamin would equally be disposed to reject this narrative of modernity as radical historical break without surviving remnants of the premodern. In this respect both he and Harvey stand opposed to a certain strain in modernism's self-understanding. In the seminal texts of architectural modernism – Le Corbusier's *Towards an Architecture* is exemplary in this regard – a rhetoric of radical change is comprehensively applied. And yet this does not, certainly in the case of Le Corbusier, preclude an equally passionate appeal to tradition. Indeed, *Towards an Architecture* is explicitly anti-revolutionary in social and political terms. For Benjamin, technological innovation must be wedded to progressive social transformation in order to be of genuine and profound significance. This is not to say that Benjamin naively ascribed direct social and political efficacy to innovations in construction.

As we have seen, Benjamin holds that the social effects of changes in constructive technique are subject to a time lag, such that later generations are given the task of cashing out such changes in political terms. This makes it difficult to derive any explicit theory of modernism directly from Benjamin's texts. Such a theory needs to be 'constructed'. In order to attempt such a construction I will initially focus on two architects who feature repeatedly within Benjamin's mature writings: Le Corbusier and the Austrian proto-modernist Adolf Loos. Both figures were socially conservative, so that appreciating their significance for Benjamin requires reading their written production largely against the grain of authorial intentions.

A commonality of approach in Loos and Le Corbusier that is immediately apparent in their writings is a visceral sense of being opposed to canonical practices of architectural schools of the time. This tendency is more pronounced in Loos, who never completed his official training in architecture and was in his own time at least as well known as a cultural essayist as an architect and interior designer. Loos' early essays, later brought together in the collection *Spoken into the Void* (German title *Ins Leere Gesprochen*), were originally published at a time when the Vienna Secession was hailed as the consummate expression of the modern zeitgeist. Speaking of an interior designed by the leading architectural member of the Secessionist group, Otto Wagner, Loos comments on the relation between function, style and socio-historical development:

> Are, for example, the chairs in the Otto Wagner Room beautiful? Not for me, since I don't find them comfortable to sit on. And I presume that will be true of everyone else. ... They are shaped like Greek chairs, but down the years the technique of sitting, the technique of resting has changed considerably. It has never stood still. In all nations and in all ages it was different (Loos 1998: 64).

These comments are in line with Baudelaire's sense of modernity as an ever-changing specificity of historical conditions, rather than a uniquely experimental or iconoclastic period. At the same time, Loos pointedly appeals to utility as a decisive criterion of sound manufacturing:

So every chair should be practical. If manufacturers made only practical chairs, then people would be able to furnish their rooms perfectly without the assistance of the interior designer. Perfect furniture produces perfect rooms. Therefore, as long as they are not dealing with rooms for special occasions, our upholsterers, architects, painters, sculptors, and interior designers should limit themselves to putting perfect pieces of furniture on the market (66).

In opposition to the Secession, Loos was scornful of what he saw as an appeal to Arts and Crafts principles fundamentally out of step with modern manufacturing conditions. Speaking of the German *Werkbund* a decade later, Loos repeated his attack against what he viewed as a profoundly contradictory attempt to produce according to supposedly timeless principles of good design. As he tersely expresses it: 'The aim of the *Werkbund* is to make things, not in the style of our times but that will last forever. That is bad' (163). In his most renowned essay, 'Ornament and Crime' from 1908, Loos formulates the principle that underlies many of his critical writings: '*the evolution of culture is synonymous with the removal of ornamentation from everyday use*' (167). On the basis of this principle Loos launched his excoriating attacks on those movements of *fin de siècle* architecture and design that sought to reintroduce the principle of handcrafted production in a period of technologically advanced mechanical manufacturing.

Benjamin took up Loos' critique in his diagnosis of the regressive tendencies inherent in *Jugendstil*. Benjamin's affinity with Loos relates to the architect's appreciation of modernity not in terms of a uniquely modern style, but rather in Baudelaire's sense of ephemeral traces of cultural change evident within everyday material culture. As Loos expresses the idea in 1908 in opposition to the *Werkbund*:

Our carriages, our glasses, our optical instruments, our umbrellas and walking sticks, our luggage and saddlery, our silver cigarette cases and ornaments, our jewelry, and our clothes are modern. They are modern because no artist has tried to barge in and take them under his – unqualified

– tutelage. It is a fact that the cultured products of our time have nothing to do with art (155).

Benjamin's affinity with Loos relates to the architect's appreciation of modernity not in terms of a uniquely modern style, but rather in Baudelaire's sense of ephemeral traces of cultural change evident within everyday material culture.

The resonances with the position of Le Corbusier over a decade later are striking. In a characteristic passage from *Towards an Architecture*, Le Corbusier brings together the two features Loos' attitude highlights: the appeal to function and the sense that modernity expresses itself most immediately, though inconspicuously, through everyday objects of use:

> Our modern life ... has created objects: its suits, its pens, its Eversharp pencils, its typewriters, its telephones, its admirable office furniture, Saint-Gobain mirrors and 'Innovation' trunks, the Gillette razor and the English pipe, the bowler hat and the limousine, the liner and the airplane.
>
> Our era fixes its style everyday. It is right before our eyes.
>
> Eyes that do not see (Le Corbusier 2007: 151, 156).

The tension that lies at the heart of the idea of modernity shared by Loos and Le Corbusier expresses itself in terms of a conflict with contemporary rules of production: architectural design opposed to common 'artistic' architectural practice, modern design that repudiates recognized designers. This tension is inherent to the very idea of an artistic avant-garde that runs ahead of academic norms and expectations. Equally significant to this sense of modernity, however, is the appeal to largely unconscious, collective processes of material production. Both architects are convinced that modernity expresses itself in the myriad objects of everyday use, and yet see themselves as involved in a heroic effort to allow that expression to become explicitly recognized. At the same time there is a positive embrace of the precision and anonymity of large-scale mechanical production as truly progressive, in opposition to the regressive tendency of any attempt to recuperate pre-industrial handcrafts. In the early writings of Le Corbusier in particular there is a paradoxical appeal to revolutionary construction by means of a return to universal, essentially changeless tenets of geometrical proportion. This curious synthesis of innovation and conservation is clearly expressed in the final, sonorous words of *Towards an Architecture*:

> Disturbed by the reactions that act on him from every quarter, the man of today senses, on the one hand, a world that is elaborating itself regularly, logically, clearly, that produces with purity things that are useful and usable; and on the other hand, he finds himself still disconcerted, still inside the old hostile framework. This framework is his home; his city, his street, his house, his apartment rise up against him. ... A great disaccord reigns between the modern state of mind that is an injunction and the suffocating stock of centuries-old detritus ... Architecture or revolution. Revolution can be avoided (307).

This overtly anti-revolutionary message is to be understood against the backdrop of its historical context, a context in which Europe was still coming to terms with the consequences of the Russian Revolution and the more generally tumultuous political environment immediately following the First World War. Just as Baudelaire's sense of aesthetic modernity is significantly informed by the socio-political context shaped by the popular European uprisings of 1848, so too is Le Corbusier's formulation of architectural modernism deeply marked by its reaction to an environment of immediate revolutionary potential. For Benjamin, by contrast, it is a question of seeking a mutually reinforcing alignment between the artistic avant-garde and a revolutionary political perspective. For this, as we have seen, he looked not so much to Le Corbusier's architectural purism but instead to the quite different, though contemporaneous, movement of surrealism.

The domestic interior as social sanctuary

While Loos and Le Corbusier see modernity and modernism primarily through the lens of design and productive technique, Benjamin's starting point is the social situation brought about through industrial material and visual production. An important reference point for Benjamin's appreciation of modernity is the pioneering sociology of Georg Simmel. Simmel's 1903 essay 'The Metropolis and Mental Life' provides an analysis of metropolitan life by means of which the impact of the modern built environment can be gauged. Simmel's essay, following Ferdinand Tönnies' opposition of community and civil society, posits a qualitative distinction between rural or small-town life on the one hand and metropolitan existence on the other. The former is taken to be primarily personal and emotional in character, the latter impersonal and intellectual. In view of the fact that the metropolitan environment is assumed to be significantly more complex and variable than that of the country or small conurbation, the inhabitants of large cities are seen as crucially concerned to filter out superabundant external stimulation. This produces what Simmel famously called the 'blasé' metropolitan character: a kind of anonymous romantic hero, worn out by over-stimulation and so no longer able to react to what the external world presents. In words that anticipate Freud's later account of the death drive in terms of psychic entropy, Simmel explains the decisive mechanism of the metropolitan personality:

> Thus the metropolitan type – which naturally takes on a thousand individual modifications – creates a protective organ for itself against the profound disruption with which the fluctuations and discontinuities of the external milieu threaten it. ... Thus the reaction of the metropolitan person to those events is moved to the sphere of mental activity which is least sensitive and which is furthest removed from the depths of the personality (Simmel 1971: 326).

The modern metropolis thus produces in its inhabitants a pronounced tendency towards *impersonalization*. Towards the end of his essay Simmel makes the provocative but unelaborated remark that the passionate defence of individualism found in such nineteenth-century thinkers as Nietzsche should be understood as a revolt against the impersonal character of the modern metropolis. With this claim in mind we can return to Benjamin's appreciation of surrealism and to the theme of the accursed nineteenth-century domestic interior.

In Chapter 1 we saw how Benjamin recollects the sense of safety and seclusion exuded by his grandmother's bourgeois interior. Whereas Benjamin recognized that the urge to protect oneself from the modern urban environment was profoundly reactionary in nature, Loos' conception of the domestic interior clearly supports this desire for withdrawal. This leads Loos to conceive of the interior as the consummate expression of the inhabitant's personality. Any mismatch between interior and character thus becomes the principal failure of interior design:

> The people do not fit in with their rooms, nor the rooms with the people. And how could they? ... They lack any inner connection with the people who occupy them, they lack that certain something [the occupant] finds in the room of the stupid peasant, the poor laborer, the old spinster: a feeling of intimacy (Loos 1998: 58).

Here Loos seeks to set up in the personalized interior a bulwark for the individual against just such an urban condition as that characterized by Simmel in terms of overstimulation and anonymity. According to Massimo Cacciari, this concern to protect the individual inhabitant from the social conditions of modern urban environment underlies Loos' architectural principles when designing houses and expresses itself as a basic opposition between the outside and inside of the structure:

> A fundamental difference exists between the wall, which belongs to the architect, and the furnishing, the overall composition of the interior, which must ensure maximum use and transformation by the inhabitant. ... The exterior says nothing about the interior because they are two different languages, and each speaks of itself. ... The architect remains true to his

calling as long as he gives maximum voice to these differences and lets them appear in full (Cacciari 1993: 106–7).

Loos' design of a house in Paris for the leading Dadaist and close associate of the surrealists in the early 1920s, Tristan Tzara, is illustrative of his constructive principles. For his design of the original façade of the Tzara House (constructed 1925–6) Loos employed the method of regulating lines lauded by Le Corbusier in *Towards an Architecture* (see Tournikiotis 2002: 66–7). While the geometry of the golden section regulates the proportions of the exterior, no ornamentation is applied to express any symbolic function of the building. Natural light is admitted into the interior for the most part from the rear of the house, thus preserving the sense of seclusion on the street side. Here, as in all his domestic interiors, Loos carefully articulated the interior space in ways suited to the function of individual rooms. In this case the *Raumplan* (spatial plan) on the main floor consisted of a large open sitting room and a raised dining room area adjoining.

While Loos professed distaste for useless ornamentation, he was not averse to using expensive materials, most notably fine marble applied as thin sheets of wall cladding. In certain interior designs, such as those for the Löwenbach apartment (1913) and the Villa Strasser (1918–19), the extensive use of marble cladding generates a strong sense of restrained, classical opulence, precisely negating the formal spontaneity and decorative dynamism of earlier Judgenstil interiors. As Tournikiotis notes, Loos 'obeyed a liberal concept of the home: as a conservative entity, it should respond to one criterion only – the well-being of its inhabitants' (Tournikiotis 2002: 40). While Benjamin was obviously drawn to Loos' appreciation of everyday culture, he rejected the architect's anachronistic attempts to design interiors that both expressed the inhabitant's character and offered protection from the outside environment. As we have seen, Benjamin sided with the surrealist drive towards an intoxication of exposure. In this light the true task of modernist construction is to break open the protective shell of the nineteenth-century interior, rather than devising new means of realizing the reactionary desire for individualized dwelling.

The true task of modernist construction is to break open the protective shell of the nineteenth-century interior, rather than devising new means of realizing the reactionary desire for individualized dwelling.

Exorcizing the accursed interior

In contrast to Loos' written pronouncements and practical, constructive principles, for Benjamin conceiving the domestic interior as a sanctuary amid urban disturbance merely offers a belated articulation of a nineteenth-century obsession: the bourgeois interior as the consummate expression and retreat of its inhabitant. Here we again touch upon Benjamin's cardinal distinction between nineteenth-century *dwelling* and twentieth-century *housing*. Viewed in light of this distinction, Loos and Le Corbusier appear to be more in opposition than agreement: the former calling for a return to dwelling through the reconstitution of the expressive interior, and the latter insisting on the need to rid the interior of its claustrophobic decorative trappings. In 'Paris, the Capital of the Nineteenth Century' Benjamin identifies *Jugendstil* design, with its ideal of the *Gesamtkunstwerk* (total artwork), as a terminal attempt of bourgeois artistic culture to assimilate, on the aesthetic and cultural level, broader social and economic forces:

> The shattering of the interior occurs via Jugendstil around the turn of the century. Of course, according to its own ideology, the Jugendstil movement seems to bring with it the consummation of the interior. The transfiguration of the solitary soul appears to be its goal. Individualism is its theory. ... But the real meaning of Jugendstil is not expressed in this ideology. It represents the last attempted sortie of an art besieged in its ivory tower by technology (Benjamin 2002: 38).

Confronted by the relentless encroachment of mechanization into all spheres of production, Benjamin argues, *Jugendstil* attempts to reintroduce a sense of the organic by shaping new materials of construction into forms recalling 'naked vegetal nature' (ibid.). Such an effort is doomed to failure. Only in the aftermath of the destruction wrought by mobilizing modern technology to the ends of mass warfare would the realization finally take hold, that art alone could never bring social structures back into line with the forces of production. This insight was expressed most clearly through the initial efforts of Dada and subsequently by surrealism; the self-destruction of art as a separate and privileged sphere of production thereby leading to its explicit politicization.

In a fragment from the AP Benjamin characterizes modernism in terms of a tension between Le Corbusier's purism and Breton's surrealism. Whereas the former envisaged a total erasure of nineteenth-century dwelling through the precise application of modern construction practices on a mass scale, the latter exhibits awareness that the spaces of the previous century could not be so easily exorcized. In a resonant passage from 'Paris, the Capital of the Nineteenth Century', Benjamin clearly ascribes to surrealism such an insight:

> Balzac was the first to speak of the ruins of the bourgeoisie. But it was Surrealism that first opened our eyes to them. The development of the forces of production shattered the wish symbols of the previous century, even before the monuments representing them had collapsed. In the nineteenth century this development worked to emancipate the forms of construction from art, just as in the sixteenth century the sciences freed themselves from philosophy. A start is made with architecture as engineered construction (Benjamin 2002: 43).

From 1922 the German artist Max Ernst was associated with the inner circle of friends who would officially launch the surrealist movement two years later. During the period of his close association with the Paris surrealists, Ernst produced artworks that brought together realism with heterogeneous, conflicting dream images. Notable examples of such efforts were three collections of collage novels featuring nineteenth-century novel illustrations with the interpellation of bizarre, incongruous images. The first such work, *La Femme 100 Têtes* (*The Hundred-Headed Woman* or *The Woman without a Head*) from

1929, contains many scenes where nineteenth-century interiors and their inhabitants are brought together with disparate material to form bewildering, suggestive juxtapositions.

In one illustration, for example, a young woman walks in the foreground with a gigantic pigeon on her shoulder. The setting appears to be a large museum or gallery, though the space contains elements of a botanical garden with three male figures standing in a pagoda in the background. Other scenes seem to offer condensed visual allegories, the meaning of which remains elusive. One image shows a middle-aged man asleep in his armchair. The chair, however, is floating on a rough sea. Out of the water the naked arm of a woman reaches toward the man in the foreground, while in the background a vertical tower of water shoots up in front of a distant lighthouse. In such collages Ernst is clearly attempting the same kind of spontaneous and unexpected meetings of objects that Breton and Philippe Soupault had first aimed at verbally in their early 'automatic writing'.

In *Une Semaine de bonté* (*A Week of Goodness*) from 1934 (see Ernst 1976) Ernst put together his most elaborately structured collage novel. This later work is arranged according to days of the week and elements, some classical ('water' and 'fire') and others unconventional or seemingly arbitrary ('mud' and 'black'). Just as each illustration is highly ambiguous, the sense of narrative across each section is fragmentary and tenuous. It is clear that the work is guided by Breton's stated surrealist aim of sensory bewilderment. Here the sense of psychosexual tension is also heightened, with many scenes depicting naked and seemingly vulnerable women and predatory male figures who are often adorned with heads or other body parts of animals. This reflects the close affinity between surrealism and the psychoanalytic approach to human perception and experience, an approach held in high regard by Breton. In his incisive and nuanced work on surrealism, *Convulsive Beauty*, the art theorist Hal Foster accentuates the connection between Ernst's work and the Freudian theory of the death drive:

> **In *Une Semaine de bonté* especially, this melodramatic return of the repressed is registered not only in the becoming-monstrous of the figures but also in**

the becoming-hysterical of the interiors: images evocative of 'perverse' desires (e.g. sodomy, sadomasochism) erupt in these rooms, most often in the spaces of representation – in paintings or mirrors on the walls. Here the mirror as a reflection of perceptual reality, the paradigm of realist painting, becomes a window onto psychic reality, the paradigm of surrealist art (Foster 1993: 177).

Foster makes explicit connections between Benjamin's idea of the accursed nineteenth-century bourgeois interior and Ernst's efforts to expose the ghosts that continue to haunt these spaces in the twentieth-century collective unconscious. He further notes that Ernst took many of the collage elements for *Une Semaine* from old catalogues of fashionable goods. Foster draws out the connection Benjamin repeatedly made between surrealist representation and commodity obsolescence:

Such interiors were filled with carpets and drapes, statues and ornaments, all dressed up in historical styles and natural motifs. But this pseudo-aristocratic disguise could not protect the objects, let alone the owners, from industrial production. ... The fetishistic shine of these products has long since dulled; what remains are the intentions of wish and anxiety with which they were once invested. In his collages Ernst seized on these traces. As a result the objects of the nineteenth-century bourgeoisie appear there less as ruins than as phantoms (179–82).

In the material brought together under the title 'The Interior, The Trace' in the AP, it is clear that the organizing principle relates back to Benjamin's reception of Brecht's poetic idea of modern city life in terms of 'erasing the traces' of dwelling. What the modern spirit of the twentieth-century metropolis desires to erase is, as we have seen, nineteenth-century interior cosiness (in German, *Gemütlichkeit*). In one of the longest comments in the section on the interior Benjamin remarks that the nineteenth century was 'addicted to dwelling' (Benjamin 1999b: 220). He specifies the ideal of dwelling in question as being that of the shell, a form of housing that is an actual physical part of the inhabitant: '[The nineteenth century] conceived the residence as a receptacle for the person, and it encased him with all his appurtenances so deeply in the dwelling's interior that one might be reminded of the inside of a compass case' (ibid.). The objects of the same interior reflect this basic function back to the inhabitant: 'What didn't the nineteenth century invent some sort of casing for! Pocket watches, slippers, egg cups, thermometers, playing cards – and in lieu of cases, there were jackets, carpets, wrappers, and covers' (ibid.). The objects collected within the bourgeois interior thus offer representations in miniature of the underlying symbolic function of this space. Looking back at such spaces from the vantage point of the 1920s, Benjamin regards this symbolic power of the interior to have been dissipated by the subsequent passage of time:

> **The twentieth century, with its porosity and transparency, its tendency toward the well-lit and airy, has put an end to dwelling in the old sense ... Jugendstil unsettled the world of the shell in a radical way. Today this world has disappeared entirely, and dwelling has diminished: for the living, through hotel rooms; for the dead, through crematoriums (221).**

This suggestion that housing has definitely vanquished dwelling stands at odds, however, with a stronger tendency in Benjamin's thinking to view history as indefeasibly two-sided. This conception of history – regarding all moments and periods in terms of both catastrophic reality and utopian possibility – is what separates Benjamin's appreciation of modernity from the avant-garde ideology that presents technological progression in terms of historical inevitability and

This conception of history – regarding all moments and periods in terms of both catastrophic reality and utopian possibility – is what separates Benjamin's appreciation of modernity from the avant-garde ideology that presents technological progression in terms of historical inevitability and irreversibility.

irreversibility. For Benjamin, by contrast, historical understanding is above all a matter of thinking in opposition to deterministic models of progression. The task, as he put it in 'On the Concept of History', is 'to brush history against the grain' (Benjamin 2003: 392).

From individual dwelling to collective housing

If Benjamin conceives of modernism in terms of a shift from dwelling to housing, what can be said of housing in positive terms? We have seen that Benjamin positively appraises the social significance of the use of a transparent material such as glass, relating it to the revolutionary intoxication induced by surrealist practice. By the same token he does not accept the naive rhetoric of architectural modernism that calls for sweeping away all remnants of pre-modern construction through comprehensive interventions on the part of heroic architectural agents. Just as the individual must 'work through' her past by means of painstaking recollection, social emancipation requires collective consciousness-raising practices that confront the material history of bourgeois domination. Whereas Benjamin's thoughts on cinema in his artwork essay offer the most explicit account of such collective practices, the writings on cities with which we began also offer important clues.

In the essay on Naples, as we saw, the description of urban life centres on exteriority and porosity. The claustrophobia of the interior was thereby given both a geographical and a class specification: domestic closure seen as a northern European and bourgeois tendency, as opposed to the openness of the working-class Mediterranean setting. Yet porosity is invoked in the 'Naples' essay to describe an urban environment that had been to a great extent sheltered from the modern industrial forces of the economy and urban planning. What seems to have attracted Benjamin is precisely the labyrinthine chaos of the Neapolitan environment. In the case of Naples, at least, the sense of urban vibrancy experienced by Benjamin had nothing to do with the opening of interior space made possible by modern construction methods and materials. Instead, such vibrancy is ascribed to what is experienced as a permanent tendency towards public festival. The festival or carnival is traditionally a periodic event in which normal social hierarchies are overturned and an egalitarian spirit takes hold of civic life for a limited period.

While Benjamin is quite aware that a key social impact of industrialization is a more rigorous and stultifying imposition of productive roles, he clearly ascribed to modernist constructive practices the potential to disrupt the rule of instrumental rationality. While the appeal to festival in the early essay on Naples suggests a premodern antidote to specifically modern social pathologies, it also makes clear that Benjamin's positive notion of housing involves a move from the domestic interior to the urban exterior. Situating this notion within a contemporary context, we can understand it as a concern for vibrant *public space*. As is evident in Benjamin's descriptions of both Naples and Moscow, collective consumption can itself take on a festive character. In present contexts urban designers generally reject the functionalist imperative of separating residential and retail units and promote instead mixed-function density.

The main distinguishing feature of housing as opposed to dwelling, however, is an overturning of the imperative to design domestic interiors as the consummate expressions of individual inhabitants. The shell-like dwelling represents for Benjamin a false consolation, an ultimately illusory protective sanctuary against the urban condition engendered by advanced capitalism. Echoing Marx we might say: dwelling is the opiate of the ruling class. For Benjamin, such dwelling was a central wish-symbol of the nineteenth-century

The shell-like dwelling represents for Benjamin a false consolation, an ultimately illusory protective sanctuary against the urban condition engendered by advanced capitalism. Echoing Marx we might say: dwelling is the opiate of the ruling class.

bourgeoisie. His idea of housing attempts to cash out what modernist construction points to as an alternative configuration of social life beyond the fetish of individualized dwelling.

In the section of the AP headed 'On the Theory of Knowledge, Theory of Progress', Benjamin takes up Marx's idea that 'the last stage of world-historical form is *comedy*' (Marx and Engels 1978: 594). After quoting Marx at some length, Benjamin adds a single sentence of commentary: 'Surrealism is the death of the nineteenth century in comedy' (Benjamin 1999b: 467). Combining this thought with Benjamin's key idea of surrealism's mission to 'bring the immense forces of "atmosphere" concealed in [the poverty of interiors, enslaved and enslaving objects] to the point of explosion' (Benjamin 1999a: 210) draws the meaning of such comedy into sharper focus. In his 'Surrealism' essay Benjamin further clarifies the broader context of this revolutionary explosion of the interior:

> At the center of this world of things stands the most dreamed-about of [the surrealists'] objects: the city of Paris itself. But only revolt exposes its Surrealist face. ... And no face is surrealistic to the same degree as the true face of a city. No picture by de Chirico or Max Ernst can match the sharp elevations of the city's inner strongholds, which one must overrun and occupy in order to master their fate and – in their fate, in the fate of the masses – one's own (211).

As the final lines of 'Surrealism' make clear, the desire 'to win the energies of intoxication for the revolution' involves acknowledging a dialectic between technology and human society that is quite distinct from the environmental determinism typical of architectural modernism in its heroic phase. In opposition to the architecturally cleansed space of modernist sobriety, Benjamin invokes the 'image space' (*Bildraum*) of surrealist intoxication. While Benjamin follows Simmel's idea of a specific personality type produced under modern urban conditions, he equally insists on the need for collective appropriation of such conditions through artistic mediation. Such mediation is needed to place modern technology at the service of a genuinely popular revolutionary change of social organization. Modernist architects such as Le Corbusier sought to promote technological innovation to support given social structures. For Benjamin, by contrast, it is a question of seizing hold of technological revolution as a material precondition of social revolution.

Interestingly, in the key instances where he identifies revolutionary potential in applications of technology within the arts, Benjamin does not speak of revolutionary class-consciousness so much as changes in collective habits. Just as Simmel rests his social psychology on a conception of the 'nerve-life' of the urban masses, Benjamin appreciates the social impact of modern technological construction in terms of collective bodily changes. Such physiological changes are seen as engendering not novel ideas but instead new collective practices. Such practices, when mediated by something akin to surrealist automatism, can bring about a revolutionary synthesis of a collective physiological state and a shared 'image space':

> The collective is a body, too. And the *physis* that is being organized for it in technology can, through all its political and factual reality, be produced only in that image space to which profane illumination initiates us. Only when in technology body and image space so interpenetrate that all revolutionary tension becomes bodily collective innervation, and all bodily innervations of the collective become revolutionary discharge, has reality transcended itself to the extent demanded by the *Communist Manifesto*. For the moment, only the Surrealists have understood its present commands (Benjamin 1999a: 217–18).

Years later, in the context of the artwork essay, Benjamin returns to this idea of revolution in terms of 'innervations of the collective' (Benjamin 2002: 124). Here, however, the immediate artistic medium in question is film. A distinction is drawn between a first phase of technology that seeks 'mastery over nature' and a second phase that aims 'rather at an interplay between nature and humanity' (107). Total adaptation to this second phase of technology, Benjamin asserts, is the condition for human emancipation, and film can be seen as a means to this end. In a fragment from 1934 Benjamin offers a clue for understanding the connection between the idea of exploding the nineteenth-century ideology of dwelling and comedy in film. Here he refers to the cinematic image of Chaplin as 'the plowshare that cuts through the masses; laughter loosens up the mass' (Benjamin 1999a: 792). In the artwork essay, we recall, a regressive collective attitude towards a Picasso painting is contrasted to 'a highly progressive reaction to a Chaplin film' (Benjamin 2002: 116). This suggests that the surrealist collage or montage would have to attain the popularity of a Chaplin film in order to bring about the collective catharsis needed to rid the social body of its outmoded attachment to the nineteenth-century wish-image of dwelling.

While purist architecture appears to offer little in the way of comedy, surrealism for its part remained largely an esoteric enclave of the artistic avant-garde. The question for a revolutionary art thus becomes: how can the emancipating transformation of the material environment promised by architectural modernism be combined with the surrealist comedy of collage? For Benjamin, the answer lies in the past rather than the future. For such a fusion had already occurred 100 years before either purism or surrealism came on the scene: in the Paris arcades of the early nineteenth century.

The question for a revolutionary art thus becomes: how can the emancipating transformation of the material environment promised by architectural modernism be combined with the surrealist comedy of collage?

The image of the city

Modernism in Benjamin is thus grasped dialectically: purism and surrealism, evolution and revolution, sobriety and intoxication, tragic elitism and comedic populism. But Benjamin's sense of this dialectic does not point to a resultant synthesis that would permanently resolve the tension between the opposed terms. The point is not to resolve the tension between purism and surrealism but rather to sharpen it. As tempting as it may be to assume the contrary, however, Benjamin is not a precursor of Robert Venturi's postmodern 'both-and' approach that sets itself directly at odds with modernism's apparent 'either-or' (Venturi 2002: 16). As we have seen, Benjamin invested heavily in the political aspirations of the artistic avant-garde and, as his reception of Giedion attests, this included architectural modernism. Benjamin's distance from modernist architecture clearly relates more to its self-understanding than to its actual practice. To some extent this sense of distance can be ascribed to the need of pioneering modernist architects to strike a polemical tone in their address to the public and the architectural academy. As indicated in the introduction to this chapter, the meaning of modernism is still a matter of lively ongoing debate. Benjamin's writings offer invaluable pointers in this context.

As already noted, Benjamin attributes two basic qualities to architecture's reception: it is experienced collectively and in a state of 'distraction'. This idea of distraction does not carry any pejorative connotation but should be taken in the positive sense of an experience that is spread out, strewn (from the German root of the term 'Zer-streuung', streuen) through a social body rather than locked into the interiority of the individual perceiver. In its everyday German usage Zerstreuung means simply 'entertainment'. To the extent that architecture is an expression of modern technology, for Benjamin it must be considered Janus-faced like all material-historical processes. In spatial terms the ambiguity of architecture for Benjamin is perhaps best captured by contrasting two 'thought figures' (Denkbilder) that recur in his writings: the interior and the labyrinth. While the figure of the labyrinth carries connotations of surrealist adventure and disorientation, it is clear that the oppression of the interior can also be transposed to the public spaces of the metropolis. The most significant case of this for Benjamin is Haussmann's massive redevelopment of Paris in the wake of the 1848 uprisings. According to Benjamin's account, such urban intervention expressed 'Napoleonic imperialism' and a 'hatred of the rootless urban population', a population which thenceforth become consciously aware of its acute alienation from the city (Benjamin 2002: 42). If architecture can function to heighten consciousness of alienation, can it also have the function of positive liberation? In the terms of Benjamin's dominant thought figures: can the accursed interior be transformed into a liberating labyrinth?

In 'Berlin Chronicle' Benjamin recounts a key epiphany he experienced in Paris. In his reflective reconstruction he sees this experience as relating to the way a city weaves together memory and imagination:

> Suddenly, and with compelling force, I was struck by the idea of drawing a diagram of my life, and knew at the same moment exactly how it was to be done. With a very simple question I interrogated my past life, and the answers were inscribed, as if of their own accord, on a sheet of paper that I had with me. A year or two later, when I lost this sheet, I was inconsolable. I have never since been able to restore it as it arose before me then, resembling a series of family trees. Now, however, reconstructing its outline in thought without directly reproducing it, I would instead speak of a labyrinth. I am concerned here not with what is installed at its enigmatic center, ego or fate, but all the more with the many entrances leading into the interior. These entrances I call 'primal acquaintances'. ... So many primal relationships, so many entrances to the maze (Benjamin 1999a: 614).

Despite the loss of his 'life-diagram' we have many clues in Benjamin's writings that the architectural figure of the labyrinth was definitive for his thinking. Whereas in Proust the memory-image works backwards, recapturing a lost point in time and thereby intensifying it, the image of the labyrinth in Benjamin emanates from the past into the present. It could be likened to a primal wish-symbol or an archetype, in so far as it is neither consciously willed (it is inscribed 'of its own accord') nor strictly individual. As will be explored at length in the next chapter, such an image of space is profoundly utopian in character. For now it is a question of pursuing a possible architecture of the labyrinth.

To entertain the thought of constructing the labyrinth is already, in a certain way, to do violence to Benjamin's thought figure. The labyrinth as image is neither a reproduction of something directly perceived in the material environment nor akin to an architectural sketch or plan. Benjamin alludes to a 'diagram' not in the sense of providing instructions for use or construction, but simply to bring out the spatial nature of his image. He also explicitly says that he is not concerned with the labyrinth's 'enigmatic center, ego or fate'. His diagram is thus not a picture-puzzle or rebus, to be analytically pondered and solved. Instead, emphasis is placed on thresholds – 'so many entrances to the maze'. Grasping this approach to the urban environment in terms of points of transition from the outside can be readily contrasted with Le Corbusier's notion of the architectural plan:

> But let us confine ourselves to the question of architecture, this thing that endures over time. Looking at things from this point of view exclusively, I will begin by drawing attention to this crucial fact: a plan proceeds *from the inside out*, for a house or a palace is an organism similar to any living creature. ... Considering the impact of a work of architecture on its site, I will show that here again the *outside* is always an *inside* (Le Corbusier 2007: 216).

Benjamin's figure of the labyrinth stands in conflict with the architectural plan as understood by Le Corbusier. Seen through the thought figure of the labyrinth we must reverse the formula: *the inside is always a function of points of entrance from the outside.*

In the Paris arcades the two perspectives meet: on the one hand, in so far as they function as repositories of habitual consumption, they are 'houses or passages having no outside' (Benjamin 1999b: 406); on the other hand, they are interiors exposed to the external elements in virtue of the transparency of glass. In addition to their haunted atmosphere, what attracted the surrealists to the arcades was a sense of their constituting something like an underground city, hidden in the midst of Haussmann's imposing boulevards. In contrast to Benjamin, who reacts against its politically oppressive character, Le Corbusier expresses his admiration for 'that magnificent legacy left by a monarch to his people: the work of Haussmann under Napolean III' (Le Corbusier 1929: 93). By the time Haussmann's work of renewal began in the 1850s most of the arcades had already been constructed. Paris was thus redesigned on a grander scale and attention was drawn away from the arcades, their fashionable sheen quickly fading. As architectural structures the arcades are accordingly doubly consigned to oblivion: first, with respect to the designers and producers, the arcades go largely unrecognized by the architectural profession; and second, from the perspective of the receivers and consumers, they quickly become unfashionable and succumb to obsolescence.

When Benjamin has recourse to the figure of the labyrinth in expressing his underlying experience of the built environment, therefore, this indicates an act of retrieval rather than production. While the surrealists mourned the destruction of their beloved Passage de l'Operá, Benjamin insisted that their social function as wish-symbols of the nineteenth-century bourgeoisie had decayed long before. The Paris arcades could not, in view of their essential function as sites of intensified commodity consumption, represent for Benjamin anything other than a variation and extension of the accursed bourgeois interior. At the same time, as a key historical locus, the arcades exhibit the basic Janus-face of history: catastrophe *and* redemption.

What Benjamin's thought figure of the labyrinth teaches us about the built environment is that, like Proust's recovery of the individual's life through memories triggered by objects, collective history must first be excavated and retrieved so that another possible course of human development can become apparent. For such archaeology to be possible, however, physical traces must await discovery. In other words, the fact that the Paris arcades physically survived their decline into functional and fashionable obsolescence is vital. In the absence of such ruins Benjamin's cultural-historical investigations could never begin. In both the interior and the labyrinth such investigations proceed, like the detective stories that Benjamin loved, on the basis of circumstantial material evidence and reconstruct the situation in which the 'crimes' of history were committed. In its heroic phase, architectural modernism sought to erase the traces of the nineteenth century; surrealism to dissolve its horrors through comic reconfiguration. For Benjamin, any politically adequate approach to history would have to learn lessons from both types of transformation. The challenge is thus to deploy modern technologies of construction in the service of collective comedy or festival, thereby avoiding the futurist celebration of war and the fascist appeal to regressive nostalgia.

What Benjamin's thought figure of the labyrinth teaches us

about the built environment is that, like Proust's recovery of

the individual's life through memories triggered by objects,

collective history must first be excavated and retrieved so that

another possible course of human development can become

apparent.

The act of retrieval that connects technology and history for Benjamin must, therefore, also be related to architecture. The trajectory of such an act can be compared to the 'crooked street' of 'Berlin Childhood around 1900' (Benjamin 2002: 372–4), rather than the 'straight line' of Le Corbusier's urbanism. This cannot mean, however, that the labyrinth falls on the other side of Le Corbusier's either-or – that of the pack-donkey, who 'takes the line of least resistance' (Le Corbusier 1929: 5). According to this opposition, modern construction must insist on the final and total victory of the rectilinear plan, for 'a modern city lives by the straight line, inevitably. ... The curve is ruinous, difficult and dangerous; it is a paralysing thing' (10).

If Benjamin's sense of modernism takes its cue from the tension between Breton and Le Corbusier, then the figure of the labyrinth must be understood in the context of modern technology. Benjamin clearly thought that the social paradigm of isolated, individualized dwelling was obsolete. Progressive efforts in construction would thus need to be geared to mass housing, housing in which inhabitants would not desire to inscribe traces of atomized existence but instead to participate in collective festival. If we wish to project a positive image of construction on the basis of these indications, then perhaps it would be most apt to speak of a provisional, mobile or even nomadic architecture. Such an idea looks like a contradiction in terms. It invites a difficult thought experiment:

instead of architecture represented by film, imagine film reconstituted as architecture. Following this line of thought leads us directly to a consideration of the utopian dimension Benjamin ascribed to art and technology.

Benjamin clearly thought that the social paradigm of isolated, individualized dwelling was obsolete. Progressive efforts in construction would thus need to be geared to mass housing, housing in which inhabitants would not desire to inscribe traces of atomized existence but instead to participate in collective festival.

CHAPTER 4

Utopianism and Utility

The politics of utopia

As is readily apparent, a common strain of utopianism runs through seminal modernist approaches to architecture and urbanism. It could hardly be claimed, however, that modernity or modernism inaugurated this connection between architecture and utopia. As David Harvey notes:

> The figures of 'the city' and of 'Utopia' have long been intertwined. In their early incarnations, utopias were usually given a distinctive urban form and most of what passes for urban and city planning in the broadest sense has been infected (some would prefer 'inspired') by utopian models of thought (Harvey 2000: 156).

Given this rich and diverse history of utopianism in connection with the city it is important to characterize Benjamin's variety as precisely as possible, prior to connecting it with his approach to architecture. To this end we can begin with a fragment written around the time of the artwork essay, that is, the winter of 1935–6. Here the question of utopia is explicitly connected to the social impact of modern technology and the nature of revolutionary praxis. The fragment turns on a distinction between two dimensions or phases of human nature: a first, biological and somatic, and a second, technological in character. The key statement comes at the end of the fragment:

> But a twofold utopian will asserts itself in revolutions. For not only does the collective appropriate the second nature as its first in technology, which makes revolutionary demands, but those of the first, organic nature (primarily the bodily organism of the individual human being) are still far from fulfilled. These demands, however, will first have to displace the

problems of the second nature in the process of humanity's development ...
(Benjamin 2002: 135).

It is necessary to turn back to the artwork essay to make further sense of this statement. In the essay, as noted in the previous chapter, Benjamin connects the first and second human nature with two phases of technology: a first striving to master nature and a second aiming 'rather at an interplay [*Zusammenspiel*] between nature and humanity'. Benjamin's affirmation of the revolutionary potential of a modern medium such as film rests on the following proposition: 'that technology will release [human beings] from their enslavement to the powers of the apparatus only when humanity's whole constitution has adapted itself to the new productive forces which the second technology has set free' (Benjamin 2002: 108).

As we saw in the previous chapter, Benjamin's notion of a shift in aesthetic reception from individual contemplation to collective 'distraction' stems from a broader understanding of modern art and technology as tending to produce a new somatic condition or human 'physis'. Whereas pre-industrial technology was developed with the goal of meeting basic material needs, industrial technology, with its economies of scale and exponential improvements in rational efficiency, is understood as opening the way to a playful, creative relationship between humanity and nature. Benjamin's appeal to the notion of *play* (in German, *Spiel*) evokes a well-established German aesthetic lineage that can be traced back to Kant and Schiller at the end of the eighteenth century. Rather than appealing to the paradigm of the individual's productive power of imagination, however, Benjamin's idea of play positions the artwork at the interface of technology and collective revolutionary politics.

Considering this characterization from the perspective of a contemporary situation that has grown largely cynical about claims that art can be socially emancipating, it can be difficult to appreciate Benjamin's apparent optimism about the political potential of modern artworks and media. Contrary to criticism aimed at Benjamin by other Critical Theorists such as Adorno, however, he does not ascribe to artworks of any kind unmediated social and political efficacy. Rather, artworks can be thus effective only in so far as they indicate *an absence of* collective freedom, equality and genuine participation. This means that, for Benjamin, the artwork can only carry redemptive (or utopian) potential precisely because it arises in a historical context of social catastrophe. In other words, modern artistic techniques and media accrue political resonance thanks to the construction of a negative image capable of indicating how a state of society under advanced capitalism falls short of implicit desires for social justice. This is Benjamin's famous *dialectic image*, which 'unexpectedly appears to the historical subject in a moment of danger' (Benjamin 2003: 391). Dialectical images are not products of modern technology as such, but emerge out of critical appropriations of modern technological practice.

This sense of utopianism in terms of a counter-image is, formally at least, in agreement with Karl Mannheim's characterization of what he calls 'utopian consciousness'. According to Mannheim, such consciousness gives rise to presentations that envisage a transformation of 'the historically existing actual reality [*Seinswirklichkeit*] by means of counter-action [*Gegenwirkung*]' (Mannheim 1995: 172). Benjamin would almost certainly have been familiar with Mannheim's 1929 book, *Ideology and Utopia*, as well as Horkheimer's critique of it (Horkheimer 1993: 129–49). More generally, it is vital when addressing the theme of utopia in Benjamin to have some awareness of the chequered history of this notion within radical socialism in the nineteenth and twentieth centuries.

An important chapter in this history is represented by Friedrich Engel's text *Socialism: Utopian and Scientific*, first published in 1880. Referring to the early nineteenth-century utopianism of such pioneering socialists as Saint-Simon, Charles Fourier and Robert Owen, Engels remarks: 'These new social systems were foredoomed as Utopian; the more completely they were worked out in detail, the more they could not avoid drifting off into pure fantasies' (Marx and Engels 1978: 687). Pure fantasy used in this derogatory sense essentially means imaginary projections freed from any reference to the real, material dialectic of history. For Engels utopian socialism lacks a sense of such history and projects what are ultimately arbitrary reconfigurations of society, arbitrary because not grounded in the basic structures of capitalist economic development. Against this, Benjamin insists that modern technology inevitably generates traces of a largely unconscious, collective utopian will that can be consciously redeemed by future generations. A section from the late text 'On the Concept of History' connects this positive appraisal of utopianism with a need to rethink technology's relationship to nature:

> [The vulgar-Marxist conception of nature] recognizes only the progress in mastering nature, not the retrogression of society; it already displays the technocratic features that later emerge in fascism. ... Compared to this positivistic view, Fourier's fantasies, which have so often been ridiculed, proved surprisingly sound. According to Fourier, cooperative labor would increase efficiency to such an extent that four moons would illuminate the sky at night, the polar ice caps would recede, seawater would no longer taste salty, and beasts of prey would do man's bidding. All this illustrates a kind of labor which, far from exploiting nature, would help her give birth to the creations that now lie dormant in her womb (Benjamin 2003: 393–4).

Benjamin's point here seems to be that Fourier's utopianism insisted on a transformation in the organization of society to match changes brought about by technologies of production. Benjamin makes this point explicitly in 'Paris, the Capital of the Nineteenth Century'. Looking back from the more recent example of Scheerbart's utopian projection of housing in the form of a modernist *Glasarchitektur* ('Glass Architecture'), Fourier's elaborately detailed 'phalanstery' appears as a resonant precursor. As a utopian architectural projection the phalanstery presents an image of a continuous corridor city, arranged as an open network of interconnected buildings with specific communal functions. According to Benjamin, Fourier saw in the arcades 'the architectural canon' of his own structure: 'The phalanstery becomes a city of arcades' (Benjamin 2002: 34). More specifically, Fourier's utopian architecture looks forward to a realized harmonization between humanity and mechanical technology:

> The highly complicated organization of the phalanstery appears as machinery. The meshing of the passions, the intricate collaboration of *passions mechanists*

with the *passion cabaliste*, is a primitive contrivance formed – on analogy with the machine – from materials of psychology. The machinery made of men produced the land of milk and honey, the primeval wish symbol that Fourier's utopia has filled with new life (ibid.).

The connection made here between utopian architecture and wish symbols is taken by Benjamin, however, as evidence of a 'reactionary metamorphosis' of the arcades from places of intensive commodity retailing to imagined spaces of authentic collective dwelling. We have seen how, for Benjamin, the only progressive attitude towards modern material culture would be one that ceases to resist the shift from dwelling to housing. As William Curtis makes clear, a line can be drawn between Fourier's architectural vision and the garden city model of Ebenezer Howard at the end of the nineteenth century. His description of Fourier's utopia is instructive:

> [The '*phalanstère*'] was supposed to stand in a rural setting and to contain all the functions necessary to support a community of about 1,800 people, who would avoid the dangers of the 'division of labour' by spending their days developing their talents and nurturing the growth of whole, uncramped personalities. ... The various quarters (including private rooms, ballrooms, a hostelry, a library and an observatory) were to be linked by a long interior street to encourage chance contacts and to embody the idea of an egalitarian society (Curtis 2002: 242).

Links between the other leading European utopian socialist, Henri Saint-Simon, and the early urbanism of Le Corbusier can also be established. Commenting on the hierarchical organization according to social-functional role written into Le Corbusier's Ville Contemporaine projection for central Paris in 1922, Curtis notes:

> There were clearly a number of ideological components; it seems clear that Le Corbusier had absorbed the ideas of Saint-Simon, especially the conception of a benevolent élite of technocrats who would act as the agents of a progress for all. This vision of the state was embodied in the skyscrapers

at the city's core, and in the romanticization of technology implicit in both the grand treatment of the roads and the machine-age tenor of the other buildings (247).

For Benjamin, by contrast, genuinely progressive utopianism cannot simply be a matter of facilitating some 'natural progression' of modern technology. Making technology into a fetish of human progress was, in his own time, the 'solution' offered by Italian futurism and later by the fascist image of community that took root in inter-war Europe. The task was instead one of constructing counter-images, images drawn from the broken promises of earlier projections of harmonized society offered by the likes of Fourier and Saint-Simon.

David Harvey proposes a distinction between utopias of 'spatial form' and those of 'social process' that goes some way to explain the difference between Benjamin's notion of utopia and that of the utopian socialists. Following the Marxian analysis also espoused by Benjamin, Harvey identifies a basic tension in architectural utopianism in so far as it projects unchanging social harmony within a context of capitalist economic development that brings with it constant social transformation and upheaval. In Harvey's words:

> Utopias of spatial form are typically meant to stabilize and control the processes that must be mobilized to build them. In the very act of realization, therefore, the historical process takes control of the spatial form that is supposed to control it (Harvey 2000: 173).

This does not mean, however, that the articulation of space through architecture and its formal utopias should be dismissed as so much worthless ideological trash. On the contrary, for Harvey as for Benjamin, the realization of utopian imagination in the flesh of architectural projects provides vital evidence of how society is structured according to the driving forces of the capitalist global economy:

> For any materialization of free-market utopianism requires that the process come to ground someplace, that it construct some sort of place within which

it can function. How it gets framed spatially and how it produces space become critical facets of its tangible realization (177).

From Benjamin's perspective, the trick is to gain an understanding of contemporary society in terms of its *failure* to realize the utopian projects implicit in the material culture of earlier generations. The point is that such failures are inevitable for as long as the basic structures of the capitalist economy remain in place. As shown, modern technologies of production are for Benjamin the primary scene within which the dialectic of actual catastrophe and utopian redemption is played out. This brings us back to the arcades, as the places where industrialized commodity capitalism constructed its original space of realization. The arcades thus represent the privileged excavation site for traces of how commodity culture realized the initial historical phase of total social dominance.

The utopian dimension of the Paris arcades

For Benjamin the arcade can be turned to for gaining an understanding of the deep structure of nineteenth-century history for a number of reasons. First, it is the site where 'art enters the service of the merchant' (Benjamin 2002: 32). The structural and perceptual predominance of display windows means that the arcades prefigure a totally visualized environment of consumption. Here sublimated desire can never take in enough of what is apparently on offer. Rather than gaining visual mastery over the environment, the viewer is in constant danger of losing her bearings and being psychologically consumed by

The structural and perceptual predominance of display windows means that the arcades prefigure a totally visualized environment of consumption. Here sublimated desire can never take in enough of what is apparently on offer.

the array of commodities. In this connection, Benjamin ascribes significance to the fact that the first arcades constructed in the early nineteenth century were panoramas, 'views of the whole', dedicated to simulating for the viewer a situation of being present at another place and time. Just as he had noted in his writings on cities in the 1920s that modernity had realized an unnerving synthesis of the rural and urban, Benjamin sees in the panoramas a certain prefiguration of the city as landscape:

> **Announcing an upheaval in the relation of art to technology, panoramas are at the same time an expression of the new attitude towards life. The city dweller, whose political supremacy over the provinces is attested many times in the course of the [nineteenth] century, attempts to bring the countryside into town. In the panoramas, the city opens up, becoming landscape – as it will do later, in subtler fashion, for the flâneurs (Benjamin 2002: 35).**

The effect of the panoramas for the social imaginary and, by extension, for artistic representation is clear enough: henceforth 'nature' cannot carry the meaning and value of something essentially opposed to the results of human artifice. Understood in this way, Benjamin's appreciation of the arcades anticipates a claim made by Henri Lefebvre decades later: 'An *urban society* is a society that results from a process of complete urbanization. This urbanization is virtual today, but will become real in the future' (Lefebvre 2003: 1).

In addition to their being the privileged site where the artwork becomes commodity, the arcades mark a revolutionary turning point for Benjamin due to the mass deployment of certain material technologies: plate glass and cast-iron. The production techniques relating to these materials do not first arise in the context of the Industrial Revolution in Europe, but the arcades mark a turning point in their efficient application on a mass scale. In this sense, the arcades represent something of a 'vulgarization' of materials previously used sparingly due to technical difficulties and prohibitive costs. Possibly following Giedion's lead, Benjamin also alludes to the fact that mass production proceeds according to a logic of universal application of standardized construction units: the iron girder, for instance, simultaneously making possible locomotive travel on standard-gauge tracks and the construction of vast railway stations and warehouses. Once standardized mass production of iron components is achieved, modern architecture has at its disposal a basic material unit that can be subject to endless permutation and variation. Giedion's appeal to heroic modern construction articulates this thought:

> *The introduction of iron into architecture signifies the change from craftsmanship to industrial building production.* The beginnings of the new architecture can be dated to the day when the old production methods were abandoned and manufactured rolled iron replaced handwrought iron (Giedion 1995: 101).

For Giedion, the transition to industrially mass-produced iron signifies more than a mere material transformation of building, for it brings about at the same time a revolution in constructed *forms*: 'iron suggests both muscular tissue and the skeleton in a building. Iron *opens* the spaces. The wall can become a transparent glass skin. To design a load-bearing wall becomes an intolerable farce' (ibid.). Here Giedion directly paraphrases Le Corbusier: 'Use of thick walls that were once a necessity has persisted, even though thin membranes of glass or brick can enclose a ground floor surmounted by fifty stories' (Le Corbusier 2007: 149).

What is key to this shared discourse on modernist construction is the facility with which practices justified in terms of economic efficiency are accorded moral and spiritual value. Thus, just as Giedion speaks of the sense of collective liberation brought about by the use of iron and glass, Le Corbusier embraces the example of the 'pure, crisp, clear, clean, sound' architecture of contemporary liners: 'A serious architect who looks as an architect (a creator of organisms) will find in the liner a liberation from cursed enslavement to the past' (Le Corbusier 2007: 158). As Jean-Louis Cohen notes in his introduction to the recent retranslation of *Towards an Architecture*, Le Corbusier had already made clear this association between modern iron construction and social liberation in correspondence from as early as 1913 (6).

We have seen that Benjamin takes up this connection between construction in iron and glass and potential social-political emancipation. It is important to recognize, however, that his first sketches relating to the Paris arcades are dominated by a sense of these nineteenth-century structures as places of collective forgetfulness and alienation. While these sketches accentuate the highly ambiguous nature of the arcades, there is no doubt that they are experienced, above all, as *accursed places of social alienation*. This is made clear by the fragments written by Benjamin between 1928 and 1929 and brought together under the provisional title 'Paris Arcades: A Dialectical Fairyland'. In a typical description, Benjamin draws out the ambiguity of the *passage* through allusions to the reflective rather than transparent qualities of glass:

> **Paris is a city of mirrors. The asphalt of its roadways smooth as glass, and at the entrance to all bistros glass partitions. A profusion of windowpanes and mirrors in cafés, so as to make the inside brighter and to give all the tiny nooks and crannies, into which Parisian taverns separate, a pleasing amplitude. Women here look at themselves more than elsewhere, and from this comes the distinctive beauty of the Parisienne. Before any man catches sight of her, she has already seen herself ten times reflected. But the man, too, sees his own physiognomy flash by. He gains his image more quickly here than elsewhere and also sees himself more quickly merged with this, his image. Even the eyes of passersby are veiled mirrors (Benjamin 1999b: 877).**

Rather than the emancipating modernist exhilaration of the glass house, evoked by Breton in his 1928 novel *Nadja* and taken up by Benjamin in his 'Surrealism' essay (Benjamin 1999a: 209), here the intensive use of glass to mirror the modern masses creates an uncanny splitting of the collective self-image. In the 1928–9 fragments Benjamin speaks of the 'ambiguity of the arcades as an ambiguity of *space*' and characterizes this two-sided space as 'now divine, now satanic' (Benjamin 1999a: 877). Recalling the dialectic between the accursed bourgeois interior of dwelling and the profane openness of modernist glass housing, it is clear that the arcade is for Benjamin simultaneously the material and symbolic meeting point of these dialectically opposed terms.

The arcade is thus the historically unique site that offers a material symbolization of the dialectical tensions of industrialized commodity production. At the same time, however, for Benjamin the arcades carry traces of a possible collective redemption. In this latter sense, the arcades bear dream-like premonitions of a social order freed from the social pathologies induced by commodity production and consumption. However, in the period of their original construction – the first half of the nineteenth century – the arcades are 'spurious constructions, glass before its time, premature iron' (879). To put it another way, the arcades suggest answers to questions that, at the time, could not even be constructed and posed.

The arcades bear dream-like premonitions of a social order freed from the social pathologies induced by commodity production and consumption.

Benjamin's contemporary and friend Ernst Bloch was pivotal in theoretically articulating the connection between modern architecture and utopianism. Whereas *The Spirit of Utopia* from 1918 had examined expressionism and ornamentation, *The Principle of Hope* offered a more sinister reading of the 'premature' use of iron and glass in the face of European totalitarianism:

> The essential feature with which the new architecture began was openness: it broke the dark stone caves, it opened up fields of vision through light glass walls, but this will to adjustment with the outside world was undoubtedly premature. The de-internalization turned into hollowness, the southern pleasure in the outside world did not, at the present sight of the capitalist outside world, turn into happiness. For nothing good happens here in the street, in the sun; the open door, the tremendously opened windows are threatening in the age of growing fascism, the house prefers to become a fortress again, if not a catacomb. The broad view full of nothing but outside world needs an outdoors full of attractive strangers, not full of Nazis; the glass door right down to the floor really requires sunshine to peer and break in, not the Gestapo (Bloch 1995: 734).

While Benjamin would no doubt have agreed with Bloch that 'only the beginnings of another society will make genuine architecture possible' (737), he could not have easily shared such a straightforward rejection of the utopianism expressed by architectural modernism. Rather than attacking Le Corbusier's idea of the house as a 'machine for living', Benjamin sees the architectural modernist programme as an important step forward in relation to earlier attempts in the nineteenth century to smother technological innovations through the use of anachronistic decorative forms. Again, the genuinely progressive utopianism of architecture under capitalist conditions is only available to a critical interpretation that goes against the grain of explicitly designed functions. Only through such acts of interpretation can modernist architecture give rise to dialectically charged 'after-images' of a utopian situation freed from systematic oppression, injustice and alienation. In this light we can begin to understand how Benjamin appreciated the Paris arcades as profoundly ambiguous carriers of utopian promise.

Rather than being universally accessible spaces, the arcades were in reality an externalized drawing room of the bourgeoisie, and as such effectively an extrusion of the accursed interior into the metropolitan exterior. Unlike the porosity Benjamin and Lacis found in the working-class neighbourhoods of Naples, where a movement from the domestic interior to the public exterior was taken to produce a sense of permanent festival, here the urban environment is transformed into the immobilized still life or 'dead nature' (*nature morte*) of the bourgeois domestic space. Just as Marx correlated the commodity fetish to frozen, thing-like social relations, so Benjamin connects the dialectical images arising out of his critical confrontation with the Paris arcades with 'dialectics at a standstill'. Deciphering such images in so far as they suggest a utopian counter-movement grounded in material-historical developments is the essential task of the *Arcades Project*. Architecture carries utopian promise, therefore, not simply as an empty counterfactual possibility. It is rather that the built environment of capitalism is equally something in reality (catastrophe) and something in potential (utopia). Critical appropriation of architecture thus requires converting the collective dream implicitly carried by the architecture of the arcades into explicit, historically lucid social action:

architecture, fashion – yes, even the weather – are, in the interior of the collective, what the sensoria of organs, the feeling of sickness or health, are inside the individual. And so long as they preserve this unconscious, amorphous dream configuration, they are as much natural processes as digestion, breathing, and the like. They stand in the cycle of the eternally selfsame, until the collective seizes upon them in politics and history emerges (Benjamin 1999b: 389–90).

Utopia and the dialectical image

The space analysed by Benjamin through the medium of the dialectical image is that of the alienated material reality of nineteenth-century capitalism. This space is the modern metropolis. Within the metropolis the arcade presents Benjamin with a microcosm that prefigures the total commodification of the material-social environment of advanced capitalism. And yet the arcades could not have assumed the role they did in Benjamin's mature thinking unless they were simultaneously grasped as positive exponents of collective utopian desires.

As shown in the previous chapter, Benjamin ascribed to architectural modernism certain attempts to direct the 'revolutionary energies' freed by surrealism towards a radical transformation of the collective material environment. Paralleling his claims for the use of montage in the experimental cinema of the 1920s, modern architecture is appreciated as a pioneering effort to bring modern societies into accord with the revolution in technological production that took place in the nineteenth century. As shown, Le Corbusier sees his programme of constructive revolution as an antidote to rather than catalyst for social revolution along Marxist lines. Clearly, however, Benjamin invests utopian potential in the *practice* of modernist architecture, rather than its often openly reactionary ideology.

Standing as we do on the far side of the modernist project, it is tempting to conclude that the ideology of standardized plan and geometrical form played a pivotal role in perverting and undermining any genuine desires for social emancipation that originally motivated the protagonists of architectural modernism. David Harvey, employing a distinction introduced by Louis Marin

(Marin 1984), aligns architectural modernism with spatial form rather than spatial play. In Harvey's view, any contemporary reappraisal of utopianism in modernist architecture must come to terms with 'an acute awareness of its inner connection with authoritarianism and totalitarianism' (2000: 163). As he notes:

> All the great urban planners, engineers, and architects of the twentieth
> century set about their tasks by combining an intense imaginary of some
> alternative world (both physical and social) with a practical concern for
> engineering and re-engineering urban and regional spaces according to
> radically new designs. While some, such as Ebenezer Howard, Le Corbusier,
> and Frank Lloyd Wright set up the imaginative context, a host of
> practitioners set about realizing those dreams in bricks and concrete,
> highways and tower blocks, cities and suburbs. ... Even when critics of the
> authoritarianism and blandness of these realized utopian dreams attacked
> them, they usually did so by contrasting their preferred version of spatial play
> with the spatial orderings that others had achieved (164).

In 'Paris, the Capital of the Nineteenth Century' Benjamin explains the utopianism of the arcades in terms of traces of a 'classless society' contained in the collective unconscious:

> And the experiences of such a society – as stored in the unconscious of the
> collective – engender, through interpenetration with what is new, the utopia
> that has left its trace in a thousand configurations of life, from enduring
> edifices to passing fashions (Benjamin 2002: 33–4).

It is clear enough that Benjamin's variety of utopianism cannot easily be made consistent with a tabula rasa model of modernist urban renewal. The complexity that characterizes Benjamin's appreciation of modernism equally holds in relation to his concept of utopianism. This concept stands at odds with both the technological historical determinism typical of heroic modernism and the cultural pessimism of his Frankfurt School colleagues. Benjamin's utopianism with respect to contemporary architecture and urbanism cannot readily be aligned with either conservative neo-traditionalism nor playful deconstructivism. While it obviously has more affinities with the latter, Benjamin's political perspective and concern for intergenerational justice is not easily incorporated within the deconstructivist paradigm.

Benjamin's utopianism with respect to contemporary architecture and urbanism cannot readily be aligned with either conservative neo-traditionalism nor playful deconstructivism. While it obviously has more affinities with the latter, Benjamin's political perspective and concern for intergenerational justice is not easily incorporated within the deconstructivist paradigm.

Gaining an adequate grasp of the connections Benjamin makes between architecture and utopia ultimately requires understanding his concept of history. While utopia may be grasped as a non-place (from the Greek *outopos*) that falls outside of actual historical developments, Benjamin thinks of it as something embedded, albeit implicitly, *within* these very developments. As already indicated, however, utopia is something virtual and potential for Benjamin and never actual. Nevertheless, utopia does have an effect in so far as it motivates collective behaviour and articulates the desire for social justice. Benjamin's utopianism thus walks a tightrope: attempting to avoid, on the one hand, reducing the utopian impulse to some shared psychological content (nothing more than a collective delusion) and, on the other, naturalizing it along the lines of the typical utopias of form found in architectural history.

While Benjamin's talk of dialectical *images* suggests he tends towards the former rather than the latter extreme, the plausibility of his utopianism requires that we understand the sense of 'image' at play as precisely as possible. In

Chapter 1 the importance of the memory-image for Benjamin's thinking was made apparent. Benjamin's numerous descriptions of such images make clear that, rather than being construed as mental contents, they are understood as *materially embedded*. In other words, the ability to recollect, when considered as a social process, is *spatially* as well as temporally determined. With this close connection of memory-image and material space in mind it becomes clearer how Benjamin can privilege the built environment as the carrier of collective historical promise. We thereby gain a more exact understanding of the central concept of Benjamin's mature thought, the 'dialectical image'. Dialectical images draw out historical, utopian promise through critical confrontation with the material culture of the past:

> while the relation of the present to the past [*Vergangenheit*] is purely temporal, the relation of what-has-been [*Gewesnen*] to the now is dialectical: not temporal in nature but figural [*bildlich*]. Only dialectical images are genuinely historical – that is, not archaic – images. The image that is read – which is to say, the image in the now of its recognizability – bears to the highest degree the imprint of the critical moment on which all reading is founded (Benjamin 1999b: 463).

As we have seen, Benjamin understands the Paris arcades as intrinsically ambiguous. The German term for ambiguous, *Zweideutig*, means literally 'pointing in two directions'. While utopia is written into the fabric of modern life for Benjamin, it lies below the surface of explicit historical consciousness for the most part. When Benjamin describes ambiguity as 'the appearance of the dialectic in images, the law of dialectics at a standstill' (Benjamin 2002: 40), he is alluding to the tensions that suspend modern material culture between catastrophe and redemption, failure and promise. In another fragment Benjamin refers to the dialectical image as 'that wherein what has been comes together in a flash with the now to form a constellation' (Benjamin 1999b: 462). Again, capturing capitalist material culture within the prism of the dialectical image simultaneously opens up two opposed aspects of the arcades: first, the alienating and disorienting phantasmagoria of the field of commodity consumption; second, the space of collective play and liberation.

In earlier chapters we saw how Benjamin looked to new media of visual production (film and photography) to offer critical mediation of modern social conditions. The connection made between the dialectical image and 'dialectics at a standstill' strongly suggests that a notion of the 'snapshot' is in play. Just as film is seen as galvanizing a potentially revolutionary mass, so Benjamin sees photographic reproductions of painting, sculpture and architecture as marking a shift from individual to collective appropriation and action:

> **Such works can no longer be regarded as the products of individuals; they have become a collective creation, a corpus so vast it can be assimilated only through miniaturization. In the final analysis, mechanical reproduction is a technique of diminution that helps people to achieve control over works of art – a control without whose aid they could no longer be used (Benjamin 1999a: 523).**

The application of mechanical processes of production to the fine arts is taken to offer a crucial screen through which the genuinely collective appropriation of technology can take place. But this artistic use of technology constitutes only a *possible* means of redemption. It still needs to be drawn out through the prism of something like Benjamin's thought figures: utopian redemption can only be located in material spaces through complementary artistic-theoretical construction. It is clear, then, that what is meant by 'dialectical image' has two main aspects: the historical *object*, space or condition to which it relates; and the *act* of interpretation or construction that strives against the standard

Utopian redemption can only be located in material spaces through complementary artistic-theoretical construction.

ideological understanding of the object. While utopian potential can only be ascribed to the arcades in terms of traces, even this vestigial presence of utopia within the accursed field of capitalist production can only be made apparent through intensive and extensive efforts of countervailing interpretation. Utopia cannot be built through some unmediated imposition of the architectural plan; it can only ever be sifted from the ruins.

Architecture and utopia

Any form of utopianism implies a certain understanding of history. In Le Corbusier's early architectural manifestoes there is a clear tension between a supposed inevitability of technological progress and a strident insistence that this progress must be made to happen. Only this latter aspect of Le Corbusier's stance can explain the seeming revolutionary violence of his architectural discourse. The analogy between architectural construction and linguistic structures of communication that lies at the heart of the purist programme is not accidental. As Tafuri makes clear, even the Dadaist and surrealist efforts to interrupt rational systems of signification appealed to techniques of speaking in a radically different mode. It might therefore be said that both sides of Benjamin's modernist dialectic worked towards utopian reconfigurations of communication. In Tafuri's words:

> The systematic use of the unexpected and the technique of assemblage were brought together to form the premises of a new nonverbal language, based on improbability and what Russian formalism called 'semantic distortion.' It was therefore precisely with Dadaism that the theory of information became an instrument of visual communication (Tafuri 1976: 96).

If avant-garde movements like Dada and surrealism posed the problems and sketched possible solutions, according to Tafuri it was architectural modernism that could subsequently claim to relate these solutions to material reality. Sharing a Marxian frame of reference with Benjamin, Tafuri takes the development of capitalist production to bring with it a constant undermining of given social orders. By the early to mid-1920s, he argues, it was generally recognized that the tensions between the forces of production and social organization gained their most powerful expression in the modern metropolis. Any programme of social reformation would therefore have to focus on material reconfigurations of the urban environment. Posing as the true inheritors of the poetic utopianism of the artistic avant-garde, modernist architects could set about not just dreaming about but building utopia. In this, though, the proponents of modernism were not true agents of change but rather unwitting puppets of the ruse of history:

> [T]he planning formulated by the architectural and urban theorists [of the 1920s] likewise pointed towards something other than itself: to wit, towards a restructuring of production and consumption in general – toward a *plan for capital*, in other words. In this sense, architecture – starting with itself – mediated between realism and utopia. The utopia lay in stubbornly continuing to hide the fact that the ideology of planning could be realized only by making clear that the true Plan could only take place beyond this sector; and that, indeed, once the Plan came within the scope of the general reorganization of production, architecture and urban planning would become its objects, not its subjects (Tafuri 1998: 20–1).

In their general account of the history of modern architecture, Tafuri and Dal Co identify the housing projects carried out in Europe under the auspices of socialist municipal governments as the place where modernist utopia most tellingly collided with the realities of market dynamics. These projects can also be considered the closest contemporary instantiations of Benjamin's notion of housing. The working-class *Siedlungen* (housing estates) designed and realized by Ernst May for the city of Frankfurt between 1925 and 1930 are taken as key instances. Tafuri and Dal Co stress how the conditions for success of these projects was optimal within the context of market constraints, pointing out that from the end of the nineteenth century over 40 per cent of municipal real estate was city-owned. For the projects May adapted the approach of the architectural avant-garde to the material problems of standardized building materials and room dimensions. In terms of architectural history, May's projects are seen as offering in practical terms a certain resolution of the tension between artistic utopianism and economic realism:

> Here architecture seems to have healed the breach between the utopia of the avant-garde, with its call for a new world, and the realistic possibilities of a

democratic administration. Frankfurt – before and more than the Dessau Bauhaus – was the real testing ground for the European modern movement in architecture. But precisely because architecture had shaken off its traditional confines as a separate kind of intellectual labor, it could be evaluated at more than methodological levels. The importance of what May achieved lay above all in making clear the grave political and administrative limitations of the entire operation carried out by German social democracy in the field of urban reform (Tafuri and Dal Co 1979: 181).

The limits of realized utopianism in this case came principally in the form of rocketing prices for building materials, increasing 140–190 per cent between the pre-war period and the end of the 1920s. Thus, even though May's efforts were given full political support by municipal authorities, which themselves possessed huge tracts of high-quality land on which to build, 'the results were neutralized by the autonomous development of finance and monopoly capital' (183).

If modernist architectural utopianism proved untenable in housing estates built connected to but outside the central city, urban design 'solutions' would be all the more questionable when located at the heart of the large city. Bruno Taut, having renounced the pre-war utopianism of spiritualist expressionism, collaborated with the Berlin assessor for city development, Martin Wagner, on a series of suburban estates for the metropolis between 1925 and 1931. In the same period Ludwig Hilbersheimer published his *Grossstadtarchitektur*, arguing against the proponents of the *Siedlungen* that the metropolis could not tolerate alternative spaces of community in its midst, and would inexorably subordinate all constructed space to the same laws of development. By the early 1930s, however, political developments were about to bring about their own total 'solution' to global capitalism beyond the paradigms of architectural design.

It is useful to have such developments in European urbanism in mind when we consider Benjamin's theoretical contribution to this historical debate. While the narrative of architectural modernism after the First World War gradually divested itself of the evocations of spiritual progress common across the avant-garde in the first decades of the twentieth century, the utopian impulse actually flourished. It should be clear by now that, although he expressed enthusiasm for the revolutionary gestures of architectural purism, Benjamin proposed a sense of utopianism that was, rather paradoxically, largely backward-looking. As shown, his focus on the arcades is motivated by a desire to reclaim something of genuine political significance in the legacy of utopian socialism. While the European architects of the *Jugendstil* period are criticized for repressing the progressive potentialities of new material technologies and striving to make the house an expression of the individual personality (see Benjamin 2002: 38), the modernists after the war are praised for their efforts to explode such oppressive interiors.

Ultimately, however, this transition in architectural paradigm is clearly understood by Benjamin as effect and not cause. As the resonant phrase of 'Paris' puts it: 'The development of the forces of production shattered the wish symbols of the previous century, even before the monuments representing them had collapsed' (43). In this sense, the Paris arcades as the surrealists and later Benjamin find them represent *posthumous architecture*. Having outlived their usefulness, all the nineteenth-century arcades have to offer are traces of a utopia etched onto the fragments of a ruin: 'They are residues of a dream world ... we begin to recognize the monuments of the bourgeoisie as ruins even before they have crumbled' (43–4).

Encountering such ruins through the mediation of the dialectical image does not amount to an attempt to retrieve their lost utopia as such. This would be to keep on dreaming. Instead, it is a question of utopian 'realization': 'The realization of dream elements, in the course of waking up, is the paradigm of dialectical thinking. Thus, dialectical thinking is the organ of historical awakening' (43). Benjamin's utopianism is predicated on a 'Copernican revolution in historical perception' that consists in seeing the present in terms of unrealized desires of the past. This is quite different from any embrace of technological progressivism that attempts to prevision the future on the basis of a continuous line of development from the past through the present and beyond. It is equally distinct from the tabula rasa rhetoric of certain forms of architectural modernism.

The ruins must be conserved – not in order to understand how it really was in the past, but in order to understand what we owe the generations before us who have struggled against oppression and domination. Taking up the resonant title of a recent work by Fredric Jameson (2005), Benjamin's utopianism is thus concerned with 'archaeologies' of rather than blueprints for the construction of the future. In analogy with Benjamin's attempts to unlock the personal sense of his present state through recollecting his childhood experience, politically progressive utopianism can never be finished with working through the past.

It has been noted several times that Benjamin's appreciation of the political potential of modern art and architecture relates to their collective and somatic rather than individual and intellectual reception. It follows from this general point that any recognition of utopian potential in modern architecture will equally relate to its role in realizing what might be called a collective human physiology. Certainly, the purist paradigm appealed to this very function of architecture. As Benjamin speculates in a fragment from the AP in relation to Giedion's idea of architectural construction playing the role of the collective subconscious in the nineteenth century: 'Wouldn't it be better to say "the role of bodily processes" – around which "artistic" architectures gather, like dreams around the framework of physiological processes?' (Benjamin 1999b: 391). Again, the point is not to go on dreaming but to jolt ourselves into wakefulness.

As we saw with respect to the techniques of modern cinematic production, progressive political potential relates not so much to the content or message as to the physiological affects of a constructive medium. As any immersion in contemporary architectural and design magazines readily illustrates, architecture, like film, can generate versions of 'hyperreality' in relation to which the environment of everyday life seems drained and lifeless. Following the threads of Benjamin's thinking, however, it is clear that he does not limit architecture to this ideological function. To see nothing but materialized apologies for advanced capitalism in architecture would be to commit the cardinal sin of Benjamin's theory of history: to grasp historical development in terms of inexorable decline and degeneration.

To see nothing but materialized apologies for advanced

capitalism in architecture would be to commit the cardinal sin

of Benjamin's theory of history: to grasp historical

development in terms of inexorable decline and degeneration.

For Benjamin, the forms of the built environment in which we happen to develop as children and adults cannot but function as repositories of collective fantasies and dreams. As the work of Gaston Bachelard has shown, personal and collective imagination is necessarily localized and embedded within the immediate built environment (Bachelard 1994). Equally, designs of the good life will always give rise to imaginary cities. A key question raised by Benjamin's utopianism is whether there is any need to attempt the actual building of such places. From our discussion it is clear that any effort of this kind gains meaning through instituting frameworks through which the present generation can genuinely communicate with the hopes of past generations.

Understood in this way, all utopian architecture in Benjamin's sense would, following his famous saying, act as documentation of the barbarous monuments of civilization. Such architecture would turn on effective *participation* of the present generation in the utopian desires of the oppressed in past generations.

All utopian architecture in Benjamin's sense would, following

his famous saying, act as documentation of the barbarous

monuments of civilization. Such architecture would turn on

effective *participation* of the present generation in the utopian

desires of the oppressed in past generations.

Whether such architecture is materially possible remains an open question. In the following chapter the theme of participation offers a thread for considering more recent developments in architecture and urbanism through the lens of Benjamin's politicized aesthetics.

CHAPTER 5

Participation and Politics

The politics of participation

The previous four chapters have explored Benjamin's relevance to architecture and urban design through interrelated themes: metropolitanism, radicalism, modernism and utopianism. What should be readily apparent at this point is the extent to which Benjamin's thinking on art and architecture is regulated fundamentally by social and political concerns. Benjamin's take on modernism, for example, centres on his appraisal of the social impact of modern technology and this impact is grasped as an opportunity for revolutionary social change. So too in the case of utopianism: the utopian impulse is not rejected as the source of so many baseless flights of fancy, but rather appreciated as a necessary element of any political perspective that holds out the hope of overcoming the systemic social pathologies brought about by advanced capitalism.

In this chapter Benjamin's legacy for architecture and urbanism is addressed in line with his underlying concern for popular social action. As the essay 'The Author as Producer' most clearly expressed it, Benjamin sought to find ways to place intellectual and artistic production in the service of a broader workers' movement. The crisis that befell the intellectual class in Europe in the first half of the twentieth century was widely acknowledged by Benjamin's contemporaries. Working outside the academy from the mid-1920s on, Benjamin was better placed than most to appreciate the urgency of making theory resonate within a broader audience.

This concern for the social efficacy of theory naturally leads into the theme of this final chapter – participation. This topic is particularly apt for rounding off our discussion of Benjamin's significance for architecture. More immediately and obviously than theorists, architectural practitioners are obliged to confront public expectations and criticisms on a regular basis. While modernist urbanism in the 1920s often adopted a rather high-handed, authoritarian attitude towards the broader community impact of its designs, grassroots urban movements in the 1960s and 1970s forced architects and planners to listen to their concerns. These days it is standard practice to conduct wide-ranging public consultation to inform planning authorities of community needs. The extent to which such consultation amounts to anything that might credibly be called public participation is a key issue at stake in contemporary architecture. This chapter will offer some pointers on how Benjamin's thinking can help address the concern of participation.

In a recent essay Tim Richardson and Stephen Connelly note how contemporary approaches to architecture and urbanism are often characterized by a concern for participation:

> **Everywhere planners are being exhorted to engage actively with communities and stakeholders in the planning of urban and rural areas, at scales ranging from regions to cities, neighbourhoods and villages. Participation is now at the heart of plan-making and strategy development, as well as being an inseparable element of individual planning decisions (Richardson and Connelly 2005: 77).**

Richardson and Connelly show how this overriding concern for participation was theoretically articulated in the 1990s by Anthony Giddens with his accounts of 'Third Way' politics in the United Kingdom and through the development of 'communitarianism' in the United States by Amitai Etzioni and others (Giddens 1998; Etzioni 1996). At first glance, the participatory agenda may seem like a recent development in urban planning and architecture. It is certainly true that the seminal case of modern urban renewal, Haussmann's radical redevelopment of Paris in the 1850s and 1860s, was far from participatory in the sense of involving the consultation and consent of affected citizens and groups within civil society. Considered more closely, however, it would be misleading to speak of a complete absence of community participation even in this historically decisive instance. As David Harvey notes:

Yet while Haussmann denied the possibility of community of one sort, he strove to implant another, founded on the glory of Empire and oozing with symbols of authority, benevolence, power, and progress, to which he hoped the 'nomads' of Paris would rally ... Haussmann tried, in short, to sell a new and more modern conception of community in which the power of money was celebrated as spectacle and display on the grand boulevards, in the *grands magasins*, in the cafés and at the races, and above all in those spectacular 'celebrations of the commodity fetish,' the Universal Expositions (Harvey 2003: 235).

As Richardson and Connelly further explain, the contemporary theory and practice of participatory urban planning has crystallized around the notion of a communicative consensus between planning authorities on the one hand and affected individuals, groups and 'stakeholders' in civil society on the other. How such consensus is best arrived at in concrete cases raises in turn difficult questions. One thing is for sure: anything approximating genuinely popular, grassroots participation in architectural design and implementation is extremely hard to achieve in practice. What does Benjamin's thinking have to offer in light of this problem?

A promising place to start addressing this question is the text 'The Author as Producer'. This essay, originally presented by Benjamin in April 1934 at the meeting of an anti-fascist group in Paris, imposes one basic demand upon the writer:

the demand *to think*, to reflect on his position in the process of production. We may depend on it: this reflection leads, sooner or later, for the writers who *matter* (that is, for the best technicians in their field), to observations that provide the most factual observation for solidarity with the proletariat (Benjamin 1999a: 779).

Here Benjamin takes it for granted that writers – also artists and intellectuals more generally – belong to the bourgeois class, by dint of the fact that they are specialized producers. Their solidarity or participation with the proletariat cannot be achieved directly, but rather 'can only be a mediated one' (780). The author is considered a specialized producer of intellectual goods, and genuine solidarity with material producers must involve the writer 'in conduct that transforms him from a supplier of the productive apparatus into an engineer who sees it as his task to adapt the apparatus to the purposes of the proletariat revolution' (ibid.). Benjamin has in mind here a key idea of his close friend, the playwright Bertold Brecht, namely the *Umfunktionierung* ('functional transformation') of the artwork. It is important to notice how Benjamin sees the committed artist as a highly skilled technician – an 'engineer' – who possesses specialized productive knowledge. In this he aligns the author with the image of the progressive architect put forward by Le Corbusier in opposition to the earlier idea of the architect as artisan, promoted by various factions of the Arts and Crafts movement.

'The Present Situation of the French Writer', an essay written some months before 'The Author as Producer', makes clear that Benjamin's direct source for his counter-image of the writer was in fact surrealism. Charting this movement's trajectory from its anarchistic beginnings in the early 1920s to its overt alignment with radical leftist politics by the end of that decade, Benjamin speaks of a development 'such that the image space which [surrealism] had so boldly opened up for itself proved more and more to be identical with the image space of political praxis' (Benjamim 1999a: 760). In this earlier essay Benjamin makes a crucial three-way connection (intellectual–technology–worker) in attempting to explain the political potential of modern artistic production: '[the surrealists] found a place for the intellectual as technologist by acknowledging the proletariat's right to make use of his technology, because only the proletariat depends on technology at its most advanced' (763).

To understand this remark and the broader connection made between artistic production and progressive political praxis, we should recall Benjamin's analyses of photography and film. The basic thought is the following: the mechanization of the means of artistic production and representation follows that of the industrialized workplace. In this workplace the collective nature of the workers is radically transformed, though consciousness of this transformation is ideologically suppressed by dint of their social position. At the same time, those among the bourgeoisie responsible for artistic and intellectual production initially resist the wholesale application of mechanical reproduction within their fields: painting is seen as threatened by the interventions of photography and the authenticity of the theatre is taken to be destroyed by the apparatus of cinematic production.

On the side of the bourgeois consumers of art there is also resistance in the form of nostalgic desire to retain a pre-mechanized image of bodily integrity, to defend it against the invasive machines of industry that threaten to cut into the pristine bodies traditionally depicted in the fine arts. As Benjamin notes: 'In the fleeting expression of a human face, the aura beckons from early photographs for the last time' (2002: 108). To have done with this nostalgia for an image of the human body prior to industrial mechanization is precisely the task of modern art: 'The alignment of reality with the masses and of the masses with reality is a process of immeasurable importance for both thinking and perception' (105).

A next stage in the movement towards complete mechanization of artistic representation is attained, as we have seen, in film. Benjamin's comparison of painting and film turns on the idea that the former calls for individual contemplation whereas the latter evokes collective 'distraction'. In both cases reception involves modes of action, but Benjamin insists that the direction of this action is reversed in the transition from non-mechanical to mechanical production: 'A person who concentrates before a work of art is absorbed by it. ... By contrast, the distracted masses absorb the work of art into themselves' (119). By absorption Benjamin essentially means *appropriation*. This process of mass absorption, Benjamin continues, is 'most obvious with regard to buildings'. It is what Benjamin calls the 'tactile' element in the mass reception of architecture that is most significant. 'Tactile reception', he explains, 'comes about not so much by way of attention as by way of habit. The latter largely determines even the optical reception of architecture, which spontaneously takes the form of casual noticing, rather than attentive observation' (120). Note that Benjamin writes of such reception of architecture not just under the conditions of industrialized modernity but 'since primeval times': '[Architecture's] history is longer than that of any other art, and its effect ought to be recognized in any attempt to account for the relationship of the masses to the work of art' (ibid.).

In the context of the artwork essay, however, Benjamin does not suggest ways in which modern architecture might allow the process of mass habitualization to become explicit. Recalling what was said about the nineteenth-century Paris arcades in earlier chapters, it is plausible to assume that Benjamin takes architectural socialization to be an intrinsically *unconscious* process. The habits induced by the built environment would, in that case, require the mediation of a further mode of artistic representation in order for them to become conscious. For Benjamin it is clearly film that performs this task. In film the conditioning induced by the workplaces of industrial capitalism is mirrored back to the workers, thereby making possible a critical reflective consciousness of the real situation of the proletariat:

> **For the majority of city-dwellers, throughout the workday in offices and factories, have to relinquish their humanity in the face of an apparatus. In the evening these same masses fill the cinemas, to witness the film actor taking revenge on their behalf not only by asserting *his* humanity (or what appears to them as such) against the apparatus, but by placing that apparatus in the service of his triumph (111).**

It is plausible to assume that Benjamin takes architectural socialization to be an intrinsically *unconscious* process. The habits induced by the built environment would, in that case, require the mediation of a further mode of artistic representation in order for them to become conscious.

Through the mediation of film the proletariat is meant not only to achieve undistorted awareness of its social position, it is also to be placed under new

conditions of action. As Benjamin characterizes the situation: 'for the first time –
and this is the effect of film – the human being is placed in a position where he
must operate with his whole living person, while forgoing its aura' (112).

Here the notion of aura must be understood in terms of its psychological effect:
the auratic image calls for rapt absorption on the part of viewers and receivers.
Ridding the represented human body of its aura allows the spell to be broken.
The camera lens acts as a medium through which viewers can subject the
represented object to continuous testing and appraisal. The film actor implicitly
understands this, Benjamin suggests, in the resistance she experiences to any
attempt to identify with her role. Like Foucault's famous descriptions of
surveillance within Bentham's panopticon, the actual absence of the viewing
public at the time of shooting the film only 'heightens the authority of their
control' over the actor (113). Clearly influenced by Brecht's methods of
dramaturgy, Benjamin sees in film 'a highly productive use of the human being's
self-alienation' (ibid.). The progressive political potential of film is not, however,
naively assumed by Benjamin regardless of broader social-political conditions:

> It should not be forgotten, of course, that there can be no political advantage
> derived from this control until film has liberated itself from the fetters of
> capitalist exploitation. Film capital uses the revolutionary opportunities
> implied by this control for counterrevolutionary purposes (ibid.).

Tafuri's critical analysis of the artistic modernism project can help us apply this
observation to twentieth-century architecture.

Architectural modernism and participation

Commenting on Le Corbusier's ideas of urbanism and the city developed in
relation to his plan to reshape Algiers in the early 1930s, Tafuri remarks:
'Architecture thus becomes a pedagogical act and a means of collective
integration' (Tafuri 1976: 132). He quotes from the architect's 1933 publication,
The Radiant City, where Le Corbusier is referring to the desired social effect of
his architectural project:

> And this deflection from the egoistic property instinct towards a feeling for collective action leads to a most happy result: the phenomenon of *personal participation* in every stage of the human enterprise. ... If you show us such plans and explain them to us, then the old dichotomy between 'haves' and 'have-nots' will disappear. There will be but a single society, united in belief and action. ... We live in an age of the strictest rationalism, and this is a matter of conscience (Tafuri 1976: 131; see Le Corbusier 1967: 177).

In the early 1920s Le Corbusier's work on private villas was complemented by projects for mass housing and a detailed programme of urbanism. In this latter area the Ville Contemporaine project from 1922 is exemplary. Designed for a population of three million and consisting of residential blocks of ten to twelve storeys on the periphery and twenty-four office towers of sixty storeys at the centre, the social ideology behind this plan is usefully summarized by Kenneth Frampton: 'Le Corbusier projected the Ville Contemporaine as an élite capitalist city of administration and control, with garden cities for the workers being sited, along with industry, beyond the "security zone" of the green belt encompassing the city' (Frampton 1992: 155). Frampton alludes to the significance of the central administrative blocks as secular replacements within the modern city for traditional religious buildings, standing as conspicuous architectural markers of social power. He also remarks on the unfavourable attention the socially repressive nature of Le Corbusier's urbanism attracted from contemporary left-wing political groups, this ideological mistrust intensifying throughout the 1920s and culminating with the 1929 Cité Mondiale project for Geneva.

In the same year Le Corbusier travelled to South America where the natural, geographical setting of Rio de Janeiro gave rise to the idea of the viaduct city. This idea came to preoccupy the architect during a four-year period of residence in Algiers between 1930 and 1933. The Obus project envisaged a massive concave structure following the natural curve of the bay, stretching for miles and consisting of six floors below and twelve above a road surface. Floors are separated by five metres and allow for internal organization by individual residents. This project stands at the centre of a period in which, according to Tafuri, 'Le Corbusier formulated the most elevated theoretical hypothesis of modern urbanism'. An achievement, Tafuri continues, that is 'still unsurpassed from the point of view of both ideology and form' (Tafuri 1976: 127). More specifically, Tafuri is here crediting Le Corbusier with having achieved, on the level of formal design, the most perfect utopian image of unified society. The project presents a fundamental synthesis of geometrical discipline and spiritual spontaneity: on the one hand, the sheer surface of vast dimensions together with the plastic grandeur of the curvilinear structure; on the other, the application of precision engineering and geometry with the invitation to individual participation in modifying residential interiors. In this way the Obus project allows for reconciliation – for Tafuri, of a purely ideological and formal nature – of the two basic elements in tension in modern technological society:

> On this scale technological structures and systems of communication must be such that they can construct a unitary *image*. ... By means of the structure of the image, and only by this means, is the reign of necessity fused with that of liberty. The former is explicated by the rigorously controlled calculations of the plan; the latter, by the recovery within it of a higher human consciousness (128–9).

Both Tafuri and Frampton draw attention to the manner in which the Algiers project represents a certain attenuation of the social authoritarianism characteristic of Le Corbusier's urbanism for most of the 1920s. Frampton refers to 'a public but pluralistic infrastructure, designed for individual appropriation, [that] was destined to find considerable currency among the anarchist architectural avant-garde of the post Second World War' (Frampton 1992: 181). The invitation to public participation in the architectural project is granted a more profoundly spiritual sense by Tafuri:

> On any level that it might be read or used, Le Corbusier's Algiers imposes a total involvement upon the public. It should be noted, however, that the participation to which the public is conditioned is a critical, reflective, and intellectual participation. An 'inattentive reading' of the urban images would produce an occult impression. And it is not to be excluded that Le Corbusier

counted on such a secondary effect as a necessary indirect stimulus (Tafuri 1976: 131).

For Tafuri the merit of the Algiers project resides in its having precisely articulated in architectural form the crisis of modern capitalist society. While he praises Le Corbusier for openly displaying the inherent tendency of this society towards totalitarian bureaucratic control, the projected resolution of such control in terms of an architectural 'conclusion' is merely ideological or, in Tafuri's terms, formal in nature. Here Tafuri takes the date of the Algiers project to be of crucial significance as it comes in the immediate wake of the world economic crisis of 1929. Following this crisis, the Keynesian theory of economic planning begins to predominate, marking an attempt to avoid future instability through rigorous efforts to regulate economic cycles and so ensure steady growth. In this way the inherent tensions of the capitalist world economy are to be ameliorated and smoothed out through innovations of architectural and urban design, rather than eliminated through revolutionary action that would fundamental change social relations in line with the forces of material production. Tafuri takes Le Corbusier at once to acknowledge the inevitable social tensions arising under capitalism and yet to offer merely formal solutions that maintain rather than challenge the capitalist logic of development. In other words, the analysis is correct but the solution false:

Le Corbusier takes account of the reality of class in the modern city and transposes the conflicts to a higher level, giving life to the most elevated proposal for the integration of the public, involved as operators and active consumers in the urban mechanism of development, now rendered organically 'human' (135).

In this way Le Corbusier's architectural project sublimates (i.e. renders ideological) the socio-economic crisis of capitalism by proposing a merely formal image of collective action and popular participation. At the same time, however, Tafuri insists that any progressive architectural aesthetic in the 1920s and 1930s could do no more than this, that is, project how the city would look if the technological capacities developed by advanced capitalist economics were subject to unified rational control.

On the basis of his comments in the artwork essay it is clear that Benjamin saw in architecture a privileged source of popular social participation through artistic mediation. In line with Giedion's idea that modernist architecture could be made intelligible only through the medium of film, Benjamin looks to artistic mediation to bring about a popular consciousness that would be aligned with revolutionary changes in construction that began 100 years before. It is vital to note that Benjamin does not simply assert this mediation of architectural reception by film without further elaboration. In fact, this claim is situated within a comprehensive interpretation of the development of visual culture under the conditions of industrialized capitalism. This development does not begin with the fine arts, but rather in connection with commodity consumption and advertising. According to Benjamin's interpretation, such things as panoramas in the early nineteenth-century inculcated in the modern urban populace new collective perceptual habits that would later allow for the mass reception of photography and cinema. Taking Paris as paradigmatic, social developments in the most industrially advanced nations during the nineteenth century are recognized as having experienced an unprecedented explosion in popular visual culture.

In quite different ways, both the unofficial architecture of the arcades and Haussmann's comprehensive urban planning are taken as radically altering the collective perceptual habits of the metropolitan population. This hybrid urban fabric – composed of both the labyrinthine architecture of the arcades and the geometrical order of Haussmann's boulevards – is precisely what, from Benjamin's perspective in the 1920s and 1930s, is to be reclaimed for popular participation through artistic mediation. In terms of their social-political origins, both of these reconfigurations of the metropolis are understood to constitute the accursed space generated by bourgeois economic dominance. Thus, the key question for Benjamin relates to identifying material means to counteract the social pathologies generated by such a built environment, and to thereby bring about collective critical consciousness or 'awakening'.

Benjamin's understanding here follows that of Lukács in *History and Class Consciousness*. As Lukács notes in his essay 'Reification and the Consciousness of the Proletariat':

it must never be forgotten: *only the practical class consciousness of the proletariat* possesses this ability to transform things. Every contemplative, purely cognitive stance leads ultimately to a divided relationship to its object. ... For every purely cognitive stance bears the stigma of immediacy. That is to say, it never ceases to be confronted by the whole series of ready-made objects that cannot be dissolved into processes. Its dialectical nature can survive only if it remains critically aware of its own tendency to immediacy inherent in every non-practical stance and if it constantly strives to explain critically the mediations, the relations to the totality as a process, to the actions of the proletariat as a class (Lukács 1971: 205).

Historically the built environment has rarely, if ever, been constructed in a genuinely popular, participatory manner. This being so, it follows that the predominant way for this environment to be experienced by most people is precisely as a 'whole series of ready-made objects'. Benjamin's sense of the politically emancipating potential of film was tied to the contingencies of his historical situation. Calling for 'the expropriation of film capital' by the proletariat in the context of European fascism seems a rather desperate gesture to us now. At the same time, however, Benjamin recognized that the film industry 'has set in motion an immense publicity machine, in the service of which it has placed the careers and love lives of the stars' (Benjamin 2002: 114). With reference to German architecture during the same period, Kathleen James-Chakraborty draws attention to a similar dualism of progressive/regressive applications:

The use of light in interwar German architecture to galvanize the emotions of a mass audience originated in an Expressionist climate of experimentation often located outside of, and at times in opposition to, the nationalist politics it would eventually serve. For [Erich] Mendelsohn light contributed to a newly egalitarian image of capitalism intended to enhance support for Germany's fragile democracy. That abstraction as a means of mass communication was unquestionably progressive from an artistic point of view did not mean, however, that it could not serve the right even more effectively that it had the left (James-Chakraborty 2000: 89).

When appraising Benjamin's aspirations for a truly participatory society we should not ascribe either too much or too little to them. On the one hand, he is not putting forward the naive view that art can, in some unmediated fashion, bring about the end of social alienation and oppression. As he himself recounts, as a young student he was caught up in widespread talk of a spiritual rebirth of Germany through art. He passed beyond such views, as did most of his contemporaries, thanks largely to the horrors of the First World War. On the other hand, only a very superficial appreciation of Benjamin's thinking on art can be arrived at when he is seen as merely offering fragments of a purely conceptual aesthetic theory. As his sustained sense of allegiance to surrealism attests, Benjamin was deeply committed to the task of placing artistic and theoretical production in the service of contemporary political efforts to counter the capitalist organization of society. Bringing the concerns of architectural design to bear on this task of redemption through artistic mediation yields intriguing results. The final sections of this chapter explore some later developments that can be seen as following the spirit of Benjamin's thinking on architecture.

Only a very superficial appreciation of Benjamin's thinking on art can be arrived at when he is seen as merely offering fragments of a purely conceptual aesthetic theory. As his sustained sense of allegiance to surrealism attests, Benjamin was deeply committed to the task of placing artistic and theoretical production in the service of contemporary political efforts to counter the capitalist organization of society.

The Situationist International and an urbanism of play

For all his sensitivity to the historical specificity of modern material technology, Le Corbusier approached the task of construction convinced of the essentially unchanging essence of human nature and society. A genuinely dialectical approach, such as the one adopted by Benjamin, recognizes by contrast that human society changes as the material environment is altered. As shown, architecture is appreciated by Benjamin as a powerful source of collective social conditioning, in the sense that it affects social behaviour in a largely unconscious manner. Architectural modernism sought to make explicit the connections between the built environment and social organization and identify strict correlations between construction and behaviour. This configuration of the technology/society relation turns largely on a drive towards *mastery* on the part of architectural agency. Benjamin suggests that the development of advanced industrial technology allows for another understanding of this relation, an alternative that turns on the idea of *play*.

Such an idea was central to the artistic-political collective known as the Situationist International (SI). The SI formed in 1957 and over a fifteen-year period formulated a critical theory and practice of everyday life that focused in its initial phase on political reconfigurations of forms of practice pioneered in the artistic avant-garde of the early twentieth century (see McDonough 2002; Knabb 2007). The core members of the group were based in Paris, though there were other groupings located across Europe. In the late 1950s, a decade before the reaction to them had become more widespread, the SI articulated a powerful critique of modernist urbanism and architecture. For example, in 'Critique of Urbanism' from 1958 the group proclaimed:

> Henceforth the crisis of urbanism is all the more concretely a social and political one, even though today no force born of traditional politics is any longer capable of dealing with it ... the bureaucratic consumer society *is here and there beginning to shape its own environment*. This society, with its new towns, is building the sites that accurately represent it, combining the conditions most suitable for its proper functioning, while at the same time

translating into spatial terms, in the clear language of the organisation of
everyday life, its fundamental principle of alienation and constraint
(McDonough 2002: 106).

Published in 1967 and credited as an important influence on the May 1968
events in Paris, Guy Debord's *The Society of the Spectacle* brought together
aspects of an analysis of consumer culture that had been offered over the
preceding decade in the SI journal. True to the original SI concern for a
'construction of situations', Debord makes clear that the point is not simply to
decry urban alienation but also to indicate what genuine urban participation
would look like:

> The proletarian revolution is that *critique of human geography* whereby
> individuals and communities must construct places and events commensurate
> with the appropriation, no longer just of their labor, but of their total
> history. By virtue of the resulting mobile space of play, and by virtue of freely
> chosen variations in the rules of the game, the independence of places will be
> rediscovered without any new exclusive tie to the soil, and thus too the
> authentic *journey* will be restored to us, along with authentic life understood
> as a journey containing its whole meaning within itself (Debord 1995: 126).

This counter-urbanist practice productive of a 'mobile space of play' originally
took the name of urban drifting or *dérive* and was initially a feature of the
pre-situationist Lettrist group from around 1953 onwards. Already as a Lettrist
activity, the *dérive* was consciously taken over from the early surrealists' habit of
wandering the less conspicuous and fashionable streets of Paris in search of
uncanny sites and chance encounters. In a text originally published in 1956 and
later included in the second issue of the SI journal in 1958, Debord sets out the
basic sense of urban drifting:

> One of the basic situationist practices is the *dérive*, a technique of rapid
> passage through varied ambiances. *Dérives* involve playful-constructive
> behavior and awareness of psychogeographical effects, and are thus quite
> different from the classic notions of journey or stroll. In a *dérive* one or more

persons during a certain period drop their relations, their work and leisure activities, and all their other usual motives for movement and action, and let themselves be drawn by the attractions of the terrain and the encounters they find there (Knabb 2007: 62).

The combination of play and construction set out by Debord echoes both Benjamin's account of the 'second technology' and also surrealism's constructive principle of mental free-association or 'psychic automatism'. As Breton made clear in the first *Surrealist Manifesto* of 1924, the revolutionary potential of modern art resides in its potential to break up established, habitual ways of responding to the material environment. The challenge thus becomes one of designing the 'space of play' that would realize genuine collective participation. This task was taken up by the Dutch artist and architect Constant Nieuwenhuys. Known simply as Constant, he was a key member of the early SI and the central figure of its Amsterdam branch, established in 1958.

In 'A Different City for a Different Life', published in the SI journal in 1959, Constant characterized situationist counter-urbanism as an urbanism of pleasure and play. More specifically, Constant's approach opposes the modernist urban schemes of zoned, radiant or garden cities and insists on the need for agglomeration, thereby arguing that the situationist counter-model – initially called 'unitary urbanism' – is above all the attempt to overcome separation and individualism through the construction of an environment built for collective play:

Instead of the idea of a garden city, which most modern architects have adopted, we set up the image of the covered city, where the layout of thoroughfares and isolated buildings has given way to a continuous spatial construction, elevated above the ground, and which will include groups of dwellings as well as public spaces (permitting modifications of purpose depending on the needs of the moment). Since all traffic, in the functional sense, will pass underneath or on overhead terraces, streets can be done away with. The great number of traversable spaces of which a city is composed form a vast and complex social space. Far from a return to nature – the notion of living in a park, as solitary aristocrats once did – we see in such immense constructions the possibility of overcoming nature and regulating at will the atmosphere, lighting, and sounds in these various spaces (McDonough 2002: 96).

Certain conspicuous modernist residues in Constant's vision, as well as a more general conviction concerning the direct social efficacy of architectural design, led to his withdrawal or expulsion (depending on which account is taken as authoritative) from the SI in 1960. In the following decade-and-a-half Constant's work centred on his New Babylon project: a vision of the environment of collective play worked out through drawings, models and sculptures. In New Babylon the built environment is constructed not according to the dictates of maximized efficiency as proposed by the protagonists of architectural modernism, but rather for the purpose of facilitating the richest variety of collective interventions on the part of inhabitants. These interventions are concretely grasped by Constant, in line with the early psychogeographical idea of creating zones with distinct emotional ambiances, as a matter of spontaneously producing and altering affective environments. With these basic concerns for general mobility and local malleability in mind Constant sets out in more concrete detail the material environment he thinks will realize the envisaged life of play:

It is a mainly horizontal skeleton, extending over ten or twenty hectares at some 15–20 meters above the ground: the total height is somewhere between 30 and 60 meters. ... A volume with the span of a New Babylon sector is more independent of the external world than a construction built on a smaller scale. Daylight, for instance, only penetrates a few meters there, a large part of the interior being artificially lit. The accumulation of solar heat and the loss of heat in cold weather occur so slowly that the changes in ambient temperature barely influence the temperature inside. The climatic conditions (the intensity of lighting, temperature, the hygrometric state, ventilation) are all under technical control. Inside, a variable range of climates can be created and modified at will. ... The audiovisual media will be used in the same spirit. The fluctuating world of the sectors calls on facilities (a transmitting and receiving network) that are both decentralized and public. Given the participation of a large number of people in the transmission and reception of images and sounds, perfected telecommunications become an important factor in ludic social behavior (Constant, 'New Babylon', www.notbored.org/new-babylon.html).

When attempting to appreciate in an adequate manner Constant's architectural utopia it is important to bear in mind that it is in fact his drawings, models and other plastic representations, rather than any theoretical account, that are in the first instance meant to communicate his vision of a society of play. These representations certainly evoke the model of the city as labyrinth, prized by Benjamin and the surrealists alike. As Andy Merrifield remarks:

> Some of Constant's plans are exhilarating, bright-colored deconstructed landscapes and plexiglass models of futuristic cities; a few actually look like giant aircraft hangars and half-finished shopping malls, massive construction sites with steel scaffolding gapping; others are sublime Piranesian labyrinths (Merrifield 2002: 99).

A recent collection of essays on the New Babylon project demonstrates how widely reactions to Constant's visualized utopia can vary (de Zegher and Wigley 2001). In his contribution, for instance, the architectural theorist Anthony Vidler favourably remarks:

> Registering the extraordinary historical and polemical effect of this unique collection of drawings, what first strikes me is the unaccountable *veracity* of Constant's project for the New Bablyon – its sense of potential realizability, or even its sense of having been already constructed (Vidler 2001: 83).

A further analysis, offered by Tom McDonough, directly challenges Vidler's affirmation of the utopian power of the diagram or visual image and identifies the role of the image in Constant as integral to his construction of a politically regressive 'architecture of presence'. McDonough speaks accordingly of a 'lingering inconsistency between Constant's aims and the actual images he created, between *New Babylon*'s theoretical critique of urbanism and an uncritical use of his media' (McDonough 2001: 99). Rather than recognizing any genuine potential for popular participation, McDonough sees in the New Babylon project a capitulation to the forces of instrumental rationality that have continued to shape the built environment of late capitalist consumption:

> In attempting to design a utopia, a no-place, Constant inadvertently prefigured our contemporary non-places: the airports, auto routes, shopping centers, and generally that whole pseudo-architecture which has come increasingly to define our everyday lives at the end of the century. ... We might say that these drawings, even at their most powerful, remain mired in contradictory language rather than embodying the language of contradiction (McDonough 2001: 100).

Benjamin, following Giedion's line of thought, ascribes to architectural construction an 'architectonic unconscious' that implicitly projects future configurations of the social environment. In this way certain architectural constructions 'dream the epoch to come'. At the same time, however, Benjamin adheres to theological and political prohibitions on attempting to predict and prefigure what is to come by means of concrete images. As he writes in a note related to the late text 'On the Concept of History':

> Whoever wishes to know what the situation of a 'redeemed humanity' might actually be, what conditions are required for the development of such a situation, and when this development can be expected to occur, poses questions to which there are no answers. He might just as well seek to know the color of ultraviolet rays (Benjamin 2003: 402).

In light of this prohibition placed on concretely predicting the future, it should be borne in mind that Constant never intended to realize his New Babylon project. Further, his images and models do correspond to two elements that have been identified as central to Benjamin's appreciation of architecture and art more generally: first, the notion of the modern metropolis as labyrinth and, second, the idea of a shift in historical phases of technology from mastery to play. Though architectural projections will always stand in tension with Benjamin's proscription on concretely envisioning the situation of redeemed humanity, Constant's representations can still be seen as a valid attempt to project an architecture of participation that follows the spirit of Benjamin's thinking.

A counter-monumental architecture of remembrance

While Constant's architecture of collective play can be taken to represent one basic dimension in Benjamin's thought (the utopian), the approach of Aldo Rossi appears appropriate to another. This second dimension is architecture's capacity to memorialize. First published in Italian in the same year that Venturi's influential *Complexity and Contradiction in Architecture* appeared in English (1966), Rossi's *The Architecture of the City* focuses on the collective and historical-political nature of the urban setting. Writing at a time when the reaction against the modernist paradigm in architecture was gathering momentum, Rossi is above all concerned with the ability of the city to articulate and transmit collective memory. While acknowledging the important role played by the urban plan, he accentuates what he calls the *singularity* of urban artefacts.

The qualitative intensity of the built environment is closely related to the memorializing function of architecture. In this connection Rossi cites the famous words of Loos' 1910 lecture on architecture: 'If we find a mound six feet long and three feet wide in the forest, formed into a pyramid, shaped by a shovel, we become serious and something in us says, "someone lies buried here." That is architecture' (Rossi 2002: 107). In fact, Loos recognizes two basic instances of architecture: the tomb (in German *Grabmal*) and the monument (*Denkmal*). As shown in earlier chapters, Benjamin's underlying purpose in the *Arcades Project* was to analyse the city of Paris by means of a new historiographical method, what he called 'the technique of awakening' (1999b: 388). Awakening, for its part, is achieved through 'the dialectical, Copernican turn of remembrance'. The German term translated as 'remembrance' is *Eingedenken*, a word related to *Gedächtnis*, meaning the power of memory in everyday German. Taken literally,

Eingedenken means simply keeping or bearing something in mind. This is the obvious function of architecture as both tomb and monument.

These connections between architecture and collective memory can be fruitfully brought into contact with Benjamin's idea, articulated in 'On the Concept of History', of documents of barbarism that accompany cultural progression under the conditions of advanced capitalism. In notes related to that text Benjamin connects the revolutionary redemption of history with the ability to gain access to 'a quite distinct chamber of the past, one which up to that point has been closed and locked' (Benjamin 2003: 402). He continues: 'The entrance into this chamber coincides in a strict sense with political action, and it is by means of such entry that political action, however destructive, reveals itself as messianic' (402).

The polemical stance of Rossi's work in relation to certain excesses of modernist functionalism is above all concerned with what he calls the singularity of cities, something he feels is derived from their respective place or locus. This singularity, he writes, 'begins *in the event and in the sign that has marked the event*' (Rossi 2002: 106). The basic problems of architecture are taken to concern 'the singularity of monuments, of the city, and of buildings, and thus the concept of singularity itself' (107). He concludes: 'All these problems are in large measure of a collective nature; they force us to pause for a moment on the relationship between place and man, and hence to look at the relationship between ecology and psychology' (ibid.).

In the previous section we encountered a similar concern for the relationship between the built environment and social action in the situationist approach. Collective awareness of the singularity of place can be readily seen as a political act of resistance when consumer culture is taken to produce a homogeneous built environment. Widely acknowledged in critical urban sociology from the early twentieth century on, this process is highlighted by Debord in *The Society of the Spectacle*:

> **Just as the accumulation of commodities mass-produced for the abstract**
> **space of the market inevitably shattered all regional and legal barriers ... so**

too it was bound to dissipate the independence and quality of *places*. The power to homogenize is the heavy artillery that has battered down all Chinese walls (Debord 1995: 120).

While the situationists remained sceptical with regard to alternative paradigms of architectural construction, Rossi asserts the permanent possibility of constructing places of genuine collective memory. Architecture, he writes, is principally concerned with the relationship between locus and design. The uniqueness of place is not, according to Rossi, an insurmountable obstacle to architectural design. Instead, the history of architecture precisely records particular responses to what is in each case a singular place. Rejecting the notion of 'context' as useful for capturing the sense of architectural design, he prefers instead the idea of the *monument*:

Beyond its historically determined existence, the monument has a reality that can be subjected to analysis; moreover, we can design a 'monument.' However, to do so requires an architecture, that is to say, a style. Only the existence of an architectural style permits fundamental choices, and from these choices the city develops (Rossi 2002: 126).

This focus on the monument leads Rossi to a basic conclusion: 'One can say that the city itself is the collective memory of its people, and like memory it is associated with objects and places' (130).

Starting with his memories of a Berlin childhood, we have seen how Benjamin's reflective experience and thought were profoundly topographical in nature. In the final phase of his writing he also became increasingly preoccupied with the idea that historical redemption could only be achieved through genuine acts of collective remembrance. In analogy with the Proustian idea that individual redemption is to be found through an encounter with objects upon which personal memories are inscribed, his wager with respect to the Paris arcades was that through remembrance of these places the social catastrophe of commodity capitalism could be redeemed. While modernism showed Benjamin that an alternative configuration of the built environment could help dispel the decay of the bourgeois interior, his encounter with surrealism convinced him that the aura of such spaces could not be exorcized so easily. The nightmare of history gives rise to texts or documents that cover over the true face of the disaster and maintain the collective torpor.

Following Benjamin's thinking, architectural monuments that resist rather than abet the given order of things must succeed in evoking concrete alternatives to the instrumentalized individualism of commodity culture. They must evoke earlier struggles that took place in the cities we continue to inhabit. The modernist imperative to construct whole cities anew was therefore rightly rejected by urban movements in the second half of the twentieth century. The only way to redeem the present, according to Benjamin's thinking, is to reclaim the suppressed potential of historically persisting places. The counter-monuments of the city, in this sense, will appear like shards that break up the tendency of the built environment to congeal into homogeneous form. They will be true reminders that what passes for the dominant reality can always be overturned through collective resistance. In Rossi's sonorous words:

The only way to redeem the present, according to Benjamin's thinking, is to reclaim the suppressed potential of historically persisting places. The counter-monuments of the city, in this sense, will appear like shards that break up the tendency of the built environment to congeal into homogeneous form. They will be true reminders that what passes for the dominant reality can always be overturned through collective resistance.

Thus the complex structure of the city emerges from a discourse whose terms of reference are still somewhat fragmentary. Perhaps the laws of the city are exactly like those that regulate the life and destiny of individual men. Every biography has its own interest, even though it is circumscribed by birth and death. Certainly the architecture of the city, the human thing par excellence, is the physical sign of this biography, beyond the meanings and the feelings with which we recognize it (Rossi 2002: 163).

CHAPTER 6

Benjamin's Memorial

Benjamin's attachment to Paris was such that he remained there through to June 1940, when he fled south to Lourdes with his sister Dora as the German army advanced through France. Having finally obtained a visa to enter the United States upon arrival at the port city of Marseilles in mid-August, the capitulation of France now meant that he could not leave the country. In late September Benjamin travelled by train to the Pyrenees and the border with Spain, his sister remaining behind in Lourdes. Together with two acquaintances he explored on foot a path through the mountains that led across the border. His health too fragile for him to return with the others to the French side of the border to rest, Benjamin spent the night of 25 September alone in the mountains. The next day, rejoined by the others, the small group entered Port Bou on the Spanish side of the border. Reporting to the town's customs office they were informed that the Spanish government had recently closed the border: they would be handed over to the French authorities the following day and almost certainly transferred to detention camps or worse.

In the early morning of 27 September Benjamin took a large dose of opium and, having asked to see her, handed a brief note to one of his companions:

> **In a situation presenting no way out, I have no other choice but to make an end of it. It is in a small village in the Pyrenees, where no one knows me, that my life will come to a close.**

The small amount of money Benjamin had with him was sufficient to rent a crypt at the local cemetery for five years. The death certificate recorded, according to his own wishes, a natural death. The name entered on the death certificate – 'Benjamin Walter' – concealed his Jewish identity and permitted burial in a Christian cemetery. After five years the tenure of the crypt lapsed and

Benjamin's body was in all likelihood removed to a mass grave. In a diary entry from May 1931, Benjamin writes of suicide:

> This willingness [to take my own life] is not the product of a panic attack; but profound though its connection is with my exhaustion from my struggles on the economic front, it would not have been conceivable without my feeling of having lived a life whose dearest wishes had been granted, wishes that admittedly I have only now come to recognize as the original text on a page subsequently covered with the handwritten marks of my destiny (Benjamin 1999a: 470).

In true fairy-tale tradition Benjamin writes of three wishes but names only one: 'the wish for distant and, above all, long journeys.' He recounts how, having exhausted his funds after fleeing Berlin for Italy in 1924, he contemplated living in a coastal cave rather than return to the city of his youth. A few days later he describes in his diary the scene that could have greeted him from his imaginary cave retreat:

> I gaze out over the landscape. Before me lies the sea, which in the bay is as smooth as a mirror; forests extend up to the hilltop, an immobile, silent mass; to one side, ruined castle walls stand there as they have for centuries; the sky is cloudless – a heavenly blue, as the phrase goes. This is what the dreamer who immerses himself in this landscape wants to see. ... To command nature herself to stand still in the name of faded images – this is the black magic of sentimentality. But to utter a call that will freeze it anew is the gift of poets (473–4).

The Israeli artist Dani Karavan has attempted his own freezing of an image with his memorial to Benjamin situated at the place of his death, Port Bou. A staircase cuts into the face of the cliff and offers a view of the sea below, framed by the sculpted passage. Karavan writes of the sea's turbulence as seen through the structure echoing the unsettled nature of Benjamin's life. On the glass sheet that separates the viewer from the sea some words of the dead man are inscribed: 'It is more arduous to honour the memory of the nameless than that of the renowned. Historical construction is devoted to the memory of the nameless.' Cacciari notes: 'Just as for Benjamin every second can reveal the "little gate" of redemption, in the same way, for Loos only a "very tiny part" of architecture can be opened to art' (1993: 196–7). No doubt Benjamin would have wished for a further inscription, repeated playfully in a letter to Hannah Arendt as an epitaph to his life as seen in its final months: 'His laziness supported him in glory for many years in the obscurity of an errant and hidden life' (Scholem and Adorno 1994: 637).

The foregoing discussion has situated Benjamin's thinking within the context of modern and contemporary architecture. As announced at the outset, the central thought that structures Benjamin's contribution to architectural theory is his recognition of a shift from dwelling to housing. Whereas dwelling functions in the work of a contemporary thinker such as Heidegger in opposition to the social impact of modern technologies of production, housing stands for the attempt to bring social practice in line with such technological production. Benjamin is one of only a handful of twentieth-century western thinkers of note who endeavoured to gauge the full social significance of modern architecture in a way that is sympathetic yet critical. His rapport with modernist art and design is equally nuanced: he recognizes the need to avoid reactionary dismissal of the avant-garde and yet acknowledges the failure of modernism to become a genuinely popular sphere of activity.

The crisis of agency that overtook western architecture in the 1970s is anticipated in a text such as 'The Author as Producer', where Benjamin calls for the intellectual and artist to move beyond their narrow sphere of technical expertise. By the same token, Benjamin admonishes against the blindness induced by heroic modernism, which in architecture calls for the razing and rebuilding of whole cities in one blow. Anticipating Rossi's notion of the city as the space of collective memory, Benjamin appeals to the idea of intergenerational justice as an antidote to heedless urban regeneration. Finally, Benjamin's thinking prefigures appeals to an architecture of play through his frequent recourse to the thought figure of the labyrinth. In this respect he again anticipates alternatives to the modernist paradigm in architecture: situationist urban drifting and psychogeography, Koetter and Rowe's idea of architectural collage, Rem Koolhaas' delirious metropolitanism and Bernard Tschumi's event cities.

This is an exciting time to engage with the work of Benjamin. While a small number of Benjamin's articles have been rightly recognized as classics for decades, theorists and practitioners are now in a uniquely strong position to gain a more rounded appreciation of Benjamin's thinking. The *Arcades Project* has been available in English for little more than a decade and the four-volume *Selected Works* was only completed in 2003. There is thus a wealth of material to be discovered and put to work in myriad areas of theory and practice. As suggested, the *Arcades Project* should be considered not so much Benjamin's *magnum opus* as a collection of deliberately untidy sketches and directions for further work. Academia's loss should be the practitioner's gain, because the very conceptual openness of Benjamin's thinking leaves space for creative critical response.

The *Arcades Project* should be considered not so much Benjamin's *magnum opus* as a collection of deliberately untidy sketches and directions for further work. Academia's loss should be the practitioner's gain, because the very conceptual openness of Benjamin's thinking leaves space for creative critical response.

It is intriguing to note that, just as Benjamin sought the historical origins of his own social situation in the mid-nineteenth century, Benjamin's mature thinking falls in a period that arguably coincides with the seminal decades that still shape current architectural and artistic culture. This suggests that the shift from dwelling to housing is something yet to reach explicit social consciousness. In a context where there are growing signs that a concern for vibrant and viable public space is becoming fundamental and urgent across many disparate social groups and sectors, Benjamin offers much to those who wish to articulate this concern effectively. While much of this book has dealt more directly with modern theory and architectural history, in the final analysis it falls to the current architectural practitioner to claim Benjamin as our posthumous contemporary.

Bibliography

Adorno, T. and Horkheimer, M. (1997) 'The Culture Industry: Enlightenment as Mass Deception', in *Dialectic of Enlightenment*, trans. J. Cumming, London/ New York: Verso.

Bachelard, G. (1994) *The Poetics of Space*, Boston: Beacon Press.

Baudelaire, C. (1964) 'The Painter of Modern Life', in *The Painter of Modern Life and Other Essays*, ed. and trans. J. Mayne, London: Phaidon.

Benjamin, W. (1986) *Moscow Diary*, ed. G. Smith, trans. R. Sieburth, Cambridge, MA: Harvard University Press.

—— (1991) *Gesammelte Schriften II*, eds R. Tiedemann and H. Schweppenhäuser, Frankfurt: Suhrkamp.

—— (1994) *The Correspondence of Walter Benjamin*, eds T. Adorno and G. Scholem, trans. M. R. Jacobson and E. M. Jacobson, Chicago: University of Chicago Press.

—— (1996) *Selected Writings*, vol. 1, eds M. Bullock and M. Jennings, Cambridge, MA: Belknap Press.

—— (1999a) *Selected Writings*, vol. 2, eds M. Jennings, H. Eiland and G. Smith, Cambridge, MA: Belknap Press.

—— (1999b) *The Arcades Project*, ed. R. Tiedemann, trans. H. Eiland and K. McLaughlin, Cambridge, MA: Belknap Press.

—— (2002) *Selected Writings*, vol. 3, eds H. Eiland and M. Jennings, Cambridge, MA: Belknap Press.

—— (2003) *Selected Writings*, vol. 4, eds H. Eiland and M. Jennings, Cambridge, MA: Belknap Press.

—— (2007) *Walter Benjamin's Archive*, eds U. Marx, G. Schwarz, M. Schwarz and E. Wizisla, trans. E. Leslie, London/New York: Verso.

Bingaman, A., Sanders, L. and Zorach, R. (2002) *Embodied Utopias: Gender, Social Change and the Modern Metropolis*, London/New York: Routledge.

Bloch, E. (1995) *The Principle of Hope*, vol. 2, trans. N. Plaice, S. Plaice and
P. Knight, Cambridge, MA: MIT Press.
—— (2000) *The Spirit of Utopia*, trans. A. Nassar, Stanford, CA: Stanford
University Press.
Boyd Whyte, I. (ed.) (2003) *Modernism and the Spirit of the City*, London/New
York: Routledge.
Breton, A. (1969) *Manifestoes of Surrealism*, trans. R. Seaver and H. Lane, Ann
Arbor, MI: University of Michigan Press.
Buck-Morss, S. (1989) *The Dialectics of Seeing: Walter Benjamin and the
Arcades Project*, Cambridge, MA: MIT Press.
—— (2006) 'The Flâneur, the Sandwichman and the Whore: The Politics of
Loitering', in *Walter Benjamin and* The Arcades Project, ed. B. Hanssen,
London/New York: Continuum.
Cacciari, M. (1993) *Architecture and Nihilism: On the Philosophy of Modern
Architecture*, trans. S. Sartarelli, New Haven/London: Yale University Press.
—— (1998) 'Eupalinos or Architecture', in *Architecture Theory since 1968*, ed.
K. Hays, Cambridge, MA: MIT Press.
Constant, 'New Babylon'. Online: www.notbored.org/new-babylon.html
(accessed 25 March 2010).
Crary, J. (1992) *Techniques of the Observer: On Vision and Modernity in the
Nineteenth Century*, Cambridge, MA: MIT Press.
—— (2001) *Suspensions of Perception: Attention, Spectacle, and Modern
Culture*, Cambridge, MA: MIT Press.
Curtis, W. (2002) *Modern Architecture since 1900*, London/New York: Phaidon
Press.
Debord, G. (1995) *The Society of the Spectacle*, trans. D. Nicholson Smith, New
York: Zone.
—— 'Theory of the Dérive' (2007) in *Situationist International Anthology*,
ed. and trans. K. Knabb, Berkeley, CA: Bureau of Public Secrets.
de Zegher, C. and Wigley, M. (eds) (2001) *The Activist Drawing: Retracing
Situationist Architectures from Constant's New Babylon to Beyond*,
Cambridge, MA: MIT Press.
Eiland, H. (2005) 'Reception in Distraction', in *Walter Benjamin and Art*,
ed. A. Benjamin, London/New York: Continuum.

Elliott, B. (2005) *Phenomenology and Imagination in Husserl and Heidegger*, London/New York: Routledge.

—— (2009) 'The Method Is the Message: Benjamin's *Arcades Project* and Theoretical Space', *International Journal of Philosophical Studies*, 17: 123–35.

—— (2010) *Constructing Community: Configurations of the Social in Twentieth-Century Philosophy and Architecture*, Lanham, MD: Lexington.

Ernst, M. (1976) *Une Semaine de Bonté: A Surrealistic Novel in Collage*, ed. S. Appelbaum, New York: Dover.

Etzioni, A. (1996) *The New Golden Rule: Community and Morality in a Democratic Society*, New York: Basic Books.

Flyvberg, B. (1998) *Rationality and Power: Democracy in Practice*, Chicago: University of Chicago Press.

Foster, H. (1993) *Compulsive Beauty*, Cambridge, MA: MIT Press.

Frampton, K. (1992) *Modern Architecture: A Critical History*, London: Thames & Hudson.

—— (1995) *Studies in Tectonic Culture: The Poetics of Construction in Nineteenth and Twentieth Century Architecture*, ed. J. Cava, Cambridge, MA: MIT Press.

Geist, J. (1985) *Arcades: The History of a Building Type*, Cambridge, MA: MIT Press.

Giddens, A. (1998) *The Third Way: The Renewal of Social Democracy*, Cambridge: Polity Press.

Giedion, S. (1995) *Building in France, Building in Iron, Building in Ferroconcrete*, trans. D. Berry, Santa Monica, CA: The Getty Center for the History of Art and the Humanities.

—— (2002) *Space, Time, and Architecture: The Growth of a New Tradition*, Cambridge, MA: Harvard University Press.

Hanssen, B. (2005) 'Benjamin or Heidegger: Aesthetics and Politics in an Age of Technology', in *Walter Benjamin and Art*, ed. A. Benjamin, London/New York: Continuum.

Harries, K. (1998) *The Ethical Function of Architecture*, Cambridge, MA: MIT Press.

Harvey, D. (1996) *Justice, Nature and the Geography of Difference*, Oxford: Blackwell.

—— (2000) *Spaces of Hope*, Berkeley/Los Angeles, CA: University of California Press.

—— (2003) *Paris, Capital of Modernity*, New York/London: Routledge.

Heidegger, M. (2008) *Basic Writings*, ed. D. Krell, San Francisco: HarperCollins.

Horkheimer, M. (1972) 'Traditional and Critical Theory', in *Critical Theory: Selected Essays*, trans. M. O'Connell *et al.*, New York: Herder & Herder.

—— (1993) 'A New Concept of Ideology?', in *Between Philosophy and Social Science*, trans. J. Torpey, Cambridge, MA: MIT Press.

Hvattum, M. and Hermansen, C. (eds) (2004) *Tracing Modernity: Manifestations of the Modern in Architecture and the City*, London/New York: Routledge.

Jacobs, J. (1993) *The Death and Life of Great American Cities*, New York: Modern Library.

James-Chakraborty, K. (2000) *German Architecture for a Mass Audience*, London/New York: Routledge.

Jameson, F. (2005) *Archaeologies of the Future: The Desire Called Utopia and Other Science Fictions*, London/New York: Verso.

Knabb, K. (2007) *Situationist International Anthology*, Berkeley, CA: Bureau of Public Secrets.

Koetter, F. and Rowe, C. (1984) *Collage City*, Cambridge, MA: MIT Press.

Koolhaas, R. (1994) *Delirious New York*, New York: The Monacelli Press.

Lahiji, N. (2005) ' "... The Gift of Time": Le Corbusier Reading Bataille', in *Surrealism and Architecture*, ed. T. Michal, London/New York: Routledge.

Le Corbusier (1929) *The City of To-morrow and Its Planning* (*Urbanisme*), London: John Rodker.

—— (1967) *The Radiant City*, New York: Orion Press.

—— (2007) *Towards an Architecture*, trans. J. Goodman, Los Angeles: The Getty Research Institute.

Lefebvre, H. (2003) *The Urban Revolution*, trans. R. Bononno, Minneapolis, MN: University of Minnesota Press.

Leslie, E. (2006) 'Ruin and Rubble in the Arcades', in *Walter Benjamin and The Arcades Project*, ed. B. Hanssen, London/New York: Continuum.

Loos, A. (1998) *Ornament and Crime: Selected Essays*, ed. A. Opel, trans. M. Mitchell, Riverside, CA: Ariadne Press.

Lukács, G. (1971) *History and Class Consciousness*, trans. R. Livingstone, Cambridge, MA: MIT Press.

McDonough, T. (2001) 'Fluid Spaces: Constant and the Situationist Critique of Architecture', in *The Activist Drawing: Retracing Situationist Architectures from Constant's New Babylon to Beyond*, eds C. de Zegher and M. Wigley, Cambridge, MA: MIT Press.

—— (ed.) (2002) 'Critique of Urbanism', in *Guy Debord and the Situationist International*, ed. T. McDonough, Cambridge, MA; MIT Press.

McLuhan, M. (1993) *Understanding Media: The Extensions of Man*, Cambridge, MA: MIT Press.

Mannheim, K. (1995) *Ideologie und Utopia*, Frankfurt: Klostermann.

Marin, L. (1984) *Utopics: Spatial Play*, London: Palgrave Macmillan.

Marx, K. and Engels, F. (1978) *The Marx–Engels Reader*, ed. R. Tucker, New York: Norton.

Merrifield, A. (2002) *Metromarxism*, New York: Routledge.

Michal, T. (ed.) (2005) *Surrealism and Architecture*, London/New York: Routledge.

Miller, T. (2006) ' "Glass before Its Time, Premature Iron": Architecture, Temporality and Dream in Benjamin's *Arcades Project*', in *Walter Benjamin and* The Arcades Project, ed. B. Hanssen, London/New York: Continuum.

Missac, P. (1995) *Walter Benjamin's Passages*, trans. S. Nicholsen, Cambridge, MA: MIT Press.

Pensky, M. (1993) *Melancholy Dialectics: Walter Benjamin and the Play of Mourning*, Amherst, MA: University of Massachusetts Press.

Pinder, D. (2005) 'Modernist Urbanism and Its Monsters', in *Surrealism and Architecture*, ed. T. Michal, London/New York: Routledge.

Polizzotti, M. (1995) *Revolution of the Mind: The Life of André Breton*, New York: Farrar Straus & Giroux.

Rendell, J. (1999) 'Thresholds, Passages and Surfaces: Touching, Passing and Seeing in the Burlington Arcade', in *The Optic of Walter Benjamin*, ed. Alex Coles, London: Black Dog Publishing.

Richardson, T. and Connelly, S. (2005) 'Reinventing Public Participation: Planning in the Age of Consensus', in *Architecture and Participation*, eds P. Blundell Jones, D. Petrescu and J. Till, London/New York: Spon Press.

Richter, G. (2006) 'A Matter of Distance: Benjamin's *One-Way Street* through *The Arcades Project*', London/New York: Continuum.

Rice, C. (2007) *The Emergence of the Interior: Architecture, Modernity, Domesticity*, London/New York: Routledge.

Rochlitz, R. (1996) *The Disenchantment of Art: The Philosophy of Walter Benjamin*, trans. J. Todd, New York/London: The Guilford Press.

Rossi, A. (2002) *The Architecture of the City*, trans. D. Girardo and J. Ockman, Cambridge, MA: MIT Press.

Scholem, G (1981) *Walter Benjamin: The Story of a Friendship*, trans. H. Zohn, New York: New York Review Books.

Scholem, G. and Adorno, T. (1994) *The Correspondence of Walter Benjamin*, trans. M. Jacobson and E. Jacobson, Chicago: University of Chicago Press.

Simmel, G. (1971) *On Individuality and Social Forms*, ed. D. Levine, Chicago: University of Chicago Press.

Sennet, R. (1994) *Flesh and Stone: The Body and the City in Western Civilization*, New York/London: Norton.

—— (2002) *The Fall of Public Man*, London: Penguin.

Sharr, A. (2007) *Heidegger for Architects*, London/New York: Routledge.

Tafuri, M. (1976) *Architecture and Utopia: Design and Capitalist Development*, trans. B. La Penta, Cambridge, MA: MIT Press.

—— (1998) 'Toward a Critique of Architectural Ideology', trans. S. Sartarelli, in *Architecture Theory since 1968*, ed. M. Hays, Cambridge, MA: MIT Press.

Tafuri, M. and Dal Co, F. (1979) *Modern Architecture*, trans. R. Wolf, New York: Harry N. Abrams.

Tönnies, F. (2001) *Community and Civil Society*, ed. J. Harris, trans. M. Hollis, Cambridge: Cambridge University Press.

Tournikiotis, P. (2002) *Adolf Loos*, New York: Princeton Architectural Press.

Venturi, R. (2002) *Complexity and Contradiction in Architecture*, New York: Museum of Modern Art.

Vidler, A. (2000) *Warped Space: Art, Architecture, and Anxiety in Modern Culture*, Cambridge, MA: MIT Press.

—— (2001) 'Diagrams of Utopia', in *The Activist Drawing: Retracing Situationist Architectures from Constant's New Babylon to Beyond*, eds C. de Zegher and M. Wigley, Cambridge, MA: MIT Press.

Witte, B. (1991) *Walter Benjamin: An Intellectual Biography*, trans. J. Rolleston, Detroit: Wayne State Press.

Wolin, R. (1994) *Walter Benjamin: An Aesthetic of Redemption*, Berkeley/Los Angeles, CA: University of California Press.

Index